HANS CHRISTIAN ANDERSEN'S

THE RED SHOES

IN A NEW VERSION BY NANCY HARRIS

World Premiere at the Gate Theatre on 6th December 2017

Our Cast

HANS CHRISTIAN ANDERSEN'S
THE RED SHOES
IN A NEW VERSION BY NANCY HARRIS

Cast (in alphabetical order)

Ensemble	Muirne Bloomer
Ensemble	Muiris Crowley
Karen/Ensemble	Stephanie Dufresne
Mags/Ensemble	Rosaleen Linehan
Prince/Ensemble	Paul Mescal
Clive/Ensemble	Robbie O'Connor
Mariella Nugent/Ensemble	Marion O'Dwyer
Sylvestor/Priest/Ensemble	David Pearse
Bob Nugent/Ensemble	Owen Roe
Ensemble	Raymond Scannell

the arts council / chomhairle ealaion | funding theatre artscouncil.ie

The Gate Theatre is grateful to The Arts Council / An Chomhairle Ealaíon for their continued support.

Writer & Cast Biographies

Writer

Nancy Harris

Gate Theatre: Debut

Other Theatre: *The Kreutzer Sonata,* (Gate Theatre, London); *One Cold Dark Night,* (Bush Theatre); *BADDIES: The Musical,* (Unicorn Theatre); *Our New Girl, Little Dolls* (Bush Theatre); *No Romance, Love in a Glass Jar,* (Peacock Theatre); *Journey to X,* (National Theatre, Connections); *The Man With The Disturbingly Smelly Foot,* (Unicorn Theatre).

Ensemble

Muirne Bloomer

Gate Theatre: *The Great Gatsby, Private Lives, Little Women, Arcadia, Dancing at Lughnasa.*

Other Theatre: *Donegal, You Never Can Tell, She Stoops to Conquer, A Doll's House, Cavalcaders, Drama at Inish, The Tempest,* (Abbey Theatre); *Dandy Dolls, Gulliver's Travels,* (Peacock Theatre); *The Train, The Making of tis a Pity She's a Whore, Wallflowering, Hue and Cry, Moment, The Star Child* (Project Arts Centre); *Rigoletto* (National Opera House and O'Reilly Theatre); *Red Riding Hood, Ssh We Have A Plan, Duck Death, The Tulip,* (Lyric Theatre); *Egg,* (Lincoln Centre NY); *Nivelli's War,* (New Victory Theatre NY); *Pinocchio, The Incredible Book Eating Boy* (The Mac); *Can You Catch a Mermaid* (Pavilion Theatre); *The Merchant of Venice,* (The Helix); *Dancing at Lughnasa,* (Bucharest National Theatre, The Helix, An Grianan); *The Death of Harry Leon,* (Smock Alley); *The Hand,* (Liberty Hall); *Laochra -GAA 1916 Centenary,* (Croke Park); *Intimate Details, Golf Swing for the Opening Ceremony of the Ryder Cup,* (K Club); *A Dash of Colour for the Opening Ceremony Special Olympics,* (Croke Park).

TV & Film: *Rock Rivals,* (ITV).

Ensemble

Muiris Crowley

Gate Theatre: *The Threepenny Opera.*

Other Theatre: *Jimmy's Hall, Oedipus, The Shadow of a Gunman, Twelfth Night, Sive, The Dead* (Abbey Theatre);

Big Maggie (Druid Theatre Company); *Elevator* (Project Arts Centre/thisispopbaby); *The Winter's Tale* (Corcadorca).

TV & Film: *Into The Badlands* (AMC); *Can't Cope Won't Cope* (Deadpan Pictures / RTÉ); *Dawn* (Neander Productions); *Smalltown* (Blank Page Productions / TV3); *Vikings* (World 2000 Entertainment / MGM); *Change in the Weather* (Tell Me Pictures); *Pilgrim Hill* (Element Pictures).

Karen/Ensemble
Stephanie Dufresne

Gate Theatre: Debut

Other Theatre: *Some Girls,*(Galway Youth Theatre); *Last Shot Redemption* (Catastrophe Theatre Company/Chrysalis Dance).

Dance: *Girlsong,* (Dublin Theatre Festival); *Changeling,* (Clonmel Junction Festival); *Space for the Liberty Muse,* (Sounds from a Safe Harbour); *Maria De Buenos Aires,* (Cork Opera House); *Makes People Talk* (Holland Dance Festival); *Ode for Seven Generators,* (Trilogy Project, Groningen); *Reworking of Blue, Body Mosaic,* (Step Up); *Windows in Progress,* (Protein Dance for The Royal Opera House); *A Darker Shade of Fado,* (NuDance and Music); *The Reason I Jump,* (Evolve);

Mags/Ensemble
Rosaleen Linehan

Gate Theatre: *Endgame, Long Day's Journey Into Night, Happy Days, Blithe Spirit, Mary Makebelieve, Heartbreak House, Season's Greetings, The Rivals, She Stoops to Conquer, Gates of Gold, Two for Joy, Twelfth Night, The Double Dealer, Absurd Person Singular.*

Other Theatre: *Beauty Queen of Leenane,* (Young Vic), *New Electric Ballroom,* (Druid); *Blood Wedding, (Almeida); Tartuffe,* (Roundabout); *Lost in Yonkers, The Plough and the Stars* (Guthrie); *Mother of All the Behans, The Importance of Being Earnest, The Mourning After Optimism* (Abbey Theatre); *Dancing at Lughnasa,* (Abbey Theatre/National Theatre); *Liolà,* (National Theatre); *Bailegangaire* (Royal Court); *Gypsy, Philadelphia here I Come, Plough and the Stars* (Gaiety Theatre).

TV & Film: *Ernestine & Kit, Moone Boy, Sharpe's Gold, Flat Lake, Happy Days, The Butcher Boy, About Adam, The Hi Lo Country,* (Working Title); *Mad About Mambo, The Assassins, Portrait of the Artist as a Young Man, Snakes and Ladders, Grushko, Suddenly Last Summer,* (BBC).

As Composer: *Speak of the Devil, Mary Makebelieve, Streets of Dublin, Des & Rosie Revues.*

Prince/Ensemble

Paul Mescal

Gate Theatre: *The Great Gatsby.*

Other Theatre: *Three Winters, Children of the Sun, Mojo, Much Ado About Nothing,* (The Lir Academy).

TV & Film: *Happyish* (DIR by Juanita Wilson).

Clive/Ensemble

Robbie O'Connor

Gate Theatre: Debut

Other Theatre: *Hentown, These Rooms, PALS, Boys of Foley Street, Laundry, World's End Lane, BASIN & Down The Valley,* (ANU Productions); *Northern Star,* (Rough Magic / UK tour); *REBEL REBEL,* (Fringe / Show in a Bag); *Hamlet,* (Second Age); *End of The Road,* (Fishamble); *All that Fall,* (Pan Pan).

TV & Film: *TinderFace,* (The Lir); *All Is By My Side,* (Watchtower Productions); *Leisure Centre,* (Desperate Optimists); *Hidden,* (BBC); *Fair City,* (RTÉ).

Mariella Nugent/Ensemble

Marion O'Dwyer

Gate Theatre: *The Heiress, The Importance of Being Earnest, Pride and Prejudice, An Ideal Husband, A Streetcar Named Desire, A Woman of*

No Importance, The Speckled People, Cat on a Hot Tin Roof, The Deep Blue Sea, Stella by Starlight, Threepenny Opera, Our Country's Good, An Ideal Husband, Twelfth Night, Fathers and Sons, Blithe Spirit, A Tale of Two Cities.

Other Theatre: *By the Bog of Cats, She Stoops to Conquer, Payback!, Bookworms, The Government Inspector, The Rivals, The Crucible, Drama at Inish, The Plough and the Stars, That Was Then, Kevin's Bed, Dancing at Lughnasa, Moving, Silver Tassie, You Can Take it with You,* (Abbey Theatre); *Be Infants in Evil, The Silver Tassie, The Loves of Cass Maguire, Lovers Meeting, The Donahue Sisters,* (Druid Theatre Co.); *Philadelphia Here I Come!,* (Lyric Theatre Belfast); *The Cavalcaders,* (Decadent Theatre Co.); *Payback!, Casanova's Limp,* (Bewley's Café Theatre); *Mrs.Whippy,* (Liberty Hall); *Big Love, En Suite, The Memory of Water* (Peacock Theatre); *Sky Road,* (Theatre Royal Waterford); *Roberto Zucco* (Bedrock); *Shadow of a Gunman, Sive,* (Tricycle Theatre); *Philadelphia Here I Come!, I do not like thee, Dr Fell, The Vagina Monologues, Juno and the Paycock,* (Gaiety Theatre); *Molly Sweeney,* (Bristol Old Vic); *From Both Hips* (Tivoli); *Wonderful Tennessee* (Broadway).

TV & Film: *Love/Hate, The Savage Eye, This is Nightlive,*

The Clinic, Finbar's Class, Secret of Ireland's Eye, (RTE); *Casualty, Ballykissangel, Rebel Heart, The Ambassador,* (BBC); *End of Sentence,* (Sentence Films DAC); *Robot Ben,* (DIT); *Covet (Siar Films); Suzie Cohen's Holy Communion,* (Underground Films); *Chasing the Green,* (Cameron Films); *Chasing the Green,* (Big Apple Productions); *Ondine,* (Ondine Productions); *Irish Jam,* (Lucky 7 Productions); *Colour me Kubrick,* (Studio Hamburg); *Agnes Brown,* (Hell's Kitchen); *Green* (Indi Films); *A Dangerous Fortune,* (Constantin TV); *Moone Boy,* (Sky); *Romantic Road,* (MOTB Productions); *Perfect Day 2 - The Funeral,* (World Productions); *Bad Crowd,* (Channel 4); *Poirot - Sad Cypress,* (Granada).

Sylvestor/Priest/Ensemble
David Pearse

Gate Theatre: *Eccentricities of a Nightingale, The Misanthrope.*

Other Theatre: *The Cripple of Inishmaan,* (Druid); *Ulysses,The Hunt For Red Willie, At Swim Two Birds, Lolita , Henry IV* (Part One), *Observe the Sons of Ulster Marching Towards the Somme,* (Abbey Theatre); *Midsummer Night's Dream,* (Barabbas); *Playboy of the Western World,* (Druid Theatre Company); *Mud,* (Corn Exchange); *Hamlet,* (Second Age); *Fileach an Fin, A Midsummer's Night Dream,* (Iomha Ildanach); *Julius Caesar, The Revenger's Tragedy,*

Measure For Measure, The Spanish Tragedy, Coriolanus and The White Devil, (Loose Canon Theatre Company); *Five, Carshow, The Seagull,* (The Corn Exchange); *Borrowed Robes, Carolan's Farewell, Pigtown,* (Island Theatre Company); *Alone It Stands,* (Yew Theatre Company); *Conversation With a Cupboard Man,* (Semper Fi); *Diarmuid and Grainne, Studs,* (Passion Machine); *Jack and the Beanstalk,* (Gaiety).

TV & Film: *Bad Day for The Cut,* (Six Mile Hill); *The Foreigner,* (STX); *The Musketeers, Rebel Heart, Bloody Sunday* (BBC); *Trivia, Bachelor's Walk, Stew,* (RTE); *Grabbers,* (Forward Films/High Treason Productions); *Moone Boy,* (Baby Cow Productions); *The Last Kingdom,* (Carnival Film & Television); *The Guard.* (Reprisal Films/ Element Pictures).

Bob Nugent/Ensemble
Owen Roe

Gate Theatre: *The Great Gatsby, One for the Road, The Father, Glengarry Glen Ross, Da, Endgame, Cat on a Hot Tin Roof, Faith Healer, Uncle Vanya, Romeo and Juliet, Great Expectations, Jane Eyre.*

Other Theatre: *Melt, Copenhagen,* (Rough Magic), *A Tender Thing* (The Project);

Sweet Bird of Youth (The Old Vic), *King Lear, The Gigli Concert, The Crucible, Six Characters in Search of an Author, The Plough and the Stars,* (The Abbey Theatre); *Skylight,* (Landmark); *Titus Andronicus,* (Siren Productions); *Heavenly Bodies, Blinded by the Light, The Mai, Prayers of Sherkin, Doldrum Bay,* (The Peacock).

TV & Film: *Undercover, The Walshes, The Shadow in the North, Inspector George Gently, Ballykissangel, Ambassadors* (BBC); *Vikings* (World 2000 / The History Channel); *Penny Dreadful* (Showtime); *Prisoners' Wives* (Tiger Aspect for ITV); *The Ice Cream Girls* (ITV); *Titanic: Blood & Steel* (3 Arts Entertainment); *Val Falvey, T.D., Wide Open Spaces* (Grand Pictures); *Prosperity* (Element Films & RTÉ); *Wait* (Independent); *Pursuit* (An Pointe Productions); *Saving the Titanic* (Tile Films); *Sensation* (Blinder Films); *Breakfast on Pluto* (Warner Bros.); *Intermission* (Company of Wolves); *Michael Collins* (Wayne Bros).

Ensemble

Raymond Scannell

Gate Theatre: *The Great Gatsby.*

Other Theatre: *Mimic, Deep,* (Self Produced); *Death at Intervals,* (Galway International Arts Festival/ Kellie Hughes);

Chekov's First Play, (Dead Centre/Tour); *Sexual Perversity in Chicago, The School For Wives, La Ronde,* (Granary Theatre); *Crave, The Heights* (Playgroup); *The Walworth Farce, The Silver Tassie,* (Druid Theatre); *Life is a Dream, Famished Castle, Digging For Fire,* (Rough Magic); *Assassins,* (SEEDS Showcase); *Infinite Lives,* (Tobacco Factory).

As Sound/Composition Designer: *Town is Dead,* (Abbey Theatre); *Alice in Funderland ,* (thisispopbaby/ Abbey Theatre); *Tasting Blue* (Megan Kennedy); *Walking Pale,* (Junk Ensemble).

Creatives Biographies

Director

Selina Cartmell

Gate Theatre:
Catastrophe, Festen, Sweeney Todd.

Other Theatre: *Fando & Lis, La Musica, Titus Andronicus, Shutter, Macbeth, Medea, The Lulu House, The Making of Tis Pity She's A Whore, A Tender Thing, Grounded* (Siren Productions); *By the Bog of Cats, King Lear, Woman and Scarecrow, Only An Apple, Big Love ,* (Abbey Theatre); *Rigoletto* (Opera Theatre Company); *Punk Rock and Three Sisters* (Lyric Theatre, Belfast) *Override* (Watford Palace, London); *The Broken Heart,* (Theatre For a New Audience, New York); *The Cordelia Dream,* (Royal Shakespeare Company); *The Prince and the Pauper,* (Unicorn Theatre); *The Giant Blue Hand,* (The Ark Theatre); *Molly Sweeney,* (Leicester Curve); *Here Lies, Passades,* (Operating Theatre, Dublin).

TV & Film: *The Date,* (RTE and Filmbase).

Set & Costume Design

Monica Frawley

Gate Theatre: *The Threepenny Opera, The London Vertigo.*

Other Theatre: *By The Bog of Cats, The Tempest, The Silver Tassie, Too Late for Logic, The Gigli Concert, Conversations on a Homecoming, Translations, The Playboy of the Western World, Juno and the Paycock,* (Abbey Theatre); *At the Black Pig's Dyke, Song of the Yellow Bittern, Dracula, Waiting for Godot,* (Druid Theatre); *The Taming of the Shrew,* (Rough Magic); *Titus Andronicus, A Tender Thing,* (Siren Productions); *Touch Me I'm Sick, Out of Harm's Way, The Wolf and Peter,* (CoisCeim Dance Theatre); *The Playboy of the Western World, Punk Rock,* (Lyric Theatre, Belfast).

Opera: *Orfeo and Eurydice, Immeneo, A Streetcar Named Desire, A Midsummer Night's Dream,* (Opera Ireland); *I Puritani,* (Staatstheater Nurenberg); *The Invader,* (Theatre Royal, Waterford).

Lighting Design
Paul Keogan

Gate Theatre: *Les Liaisons Dangereuses, The Birds, The Old Curiosity Shop, The Deep Blue Sea, Festen, Performances, The Gates of Gold, Molly Sweeney, A Streetcar Named Desire.*

Other Theatre: *Postcards from the Ledge, Breaking Dad, Between Foxrock and a Hard Place, The Walworth Farce,* (Landmark Productions Ireland); *Katie Roche, Cyprus Avenue, The Plough and The Stars, Our Few and Evil Days, The Risen People, Woman and Scarecrow, Big Love, Drum Belly,* (Abbey Theatre); *The Caretaker* (Bristol Old Vic); *A Short History of Tractors in Ukrainian, The Gaul,* (Hull Truck); *Tribes, Blasted, Afterplay, Blue/Orange,* (Crucible Sheffield); *Sinners, Here Comes The Night,* (Lyric Theatre Belfast); *A Streetcar Named Desire,* (Liverpool Playhouse); *Before it Rains,* (Sherman Cymru/Bristol Old Vic), *The Hudsucker Proxy,* (Nuffield Southampton); *Far Away,* (Corcadora Theatre Company); *Big Maggie,* (Druid, Galway); *Titus Andronicus, Shutter,* (Siren Productions); *Falstaff,* (Vienna State Opera); *Les dialogues des Carmelites,* (Grange Park Opera); *Wake,* (Nationale Reisopera, Netherlands); *The Makropulos Case,* (Opera Zuid, Netherlands); *Dead Man Walking,* (Opera Ireland); *Giselle* (Ballet Ireland); *Cassandra, Hansel and Gretel,* (Royal Ballet); *No Man's Land* (English National Ballet/Queensland Ballet).

Choreographer
Liz Roche

Gate Theatre: *Festen, The Mariner.*

Other Theatre: *Anna Karenina, DrumBelly, King Lear, Alice In Funderland, The Government Inspector,* (Abbey Theatre); *Woyzeck in Winter, The Talk of the Town, Miss Julie, The Secret Garden, Alice In Wonderland, Woyzeck in Winter, The Talk of the Town, Miss Julie and The Secret Garden* (Landmark Productions); *Dancing at Lughnasa,* (Lyric Theatre Belfast); *Bastard Amber,* (Abbey Theatre, Dublin Dance Festival and Kilkenny Arts Festival); *Medea* and *A Tender Thing for* (Siren Productions); *Embodied,* (Dublin Dance Festival).

Opera: Liz has choreographed work for Wexford Festival Opera, National Opera of Korea, Rossini Opera Festival, Opernhaus Zurich, Opera de Nice and Opera Ireland.

Composer
Marc Teitler

Gate Theatre: *Debut*

Other Theatre: *The Grinning*

Man, (Trafalgar Studios); *Baddies,* (Unicorn Theatre); *Blood and Gifts, Stuck on a Sunday, Twitterdämmerung,* (National Theatre); *Giving,* (Hampstead Theatre); *Adot;* (Royal Albert Hall); *Does my Society Look Big in This?,* (Bristol Old Vic); *The Secret Agent,* (Young Vic).

TV & Film: *Beacon 77,* (Revolt Films); *Hearts,* (dir. Thomas Strueck); *Missing,* (dir. Cristian Wiesenfeld); *Suicide Note, Private Waltz, Quercus,* (dir. Marina Waltz).

Associate Director

Maisie Lee

Gate Theatre: *Debut*

Other Theatre: *The Talk of The Town* (Dublin Theatre Festival); *Normal,* (Dublin Fringe Festival); *DNA,* (Backstage Theatre, Longford); *A Christmas Carol,* (The Ark); *Something Unspoken, Here Comes Love,* (Bewley's Café Theatre); *Heartbreak House, Aristocrats, Twelfth Night, Sive, The Risen People, Shadow of a Gunman, Future Tense* (Abbey Theatre); *Our Island, In Dog Years I'm Dead, Threshold, The Infant, 7 Jewish Children, How to be Loved,* (Mirari Productions); *Busk,* (Project Arts Centre); *The Hunt for Red Willy,* (Smock Alley Theatre); *The Tinteán Tales,* (Pearse Museum).

Radio: *Revolution Radio* (RTE 2FM), *Stepping Stones* (Walk in My Shoes Radio), *Moore than a Garden, The Silver Branch,* (Dublin South Radio).

Assistant Designer

Katie Davenport

Gate Theatre: *Red Shoes* (Designer in Residence).

Other Theatre: *What Put The Blood,* (Peacock Theatre); *Much Ado about Nothing, Mojo, Spring Awakening,* (The Lir); *Noel The Musical,* (Wexford Opera House); *From Eden,* (National Tour); *Slice the Thief,* (Boy's School); *Gordon Osram's Funeral,* (Accidental Theatre); *Signature,* (Coiscéim); *The Aeneid,* (Collapsing Horse); *Hear My Hands,* (Mermaid Arts Centre); *Dusk,* (The New Theatre).

Assistant and Associate Work: *Anna Karenina, By The Bog of Cats, The Shadow of Gunman, Suor Angelica,* (Abbey Theatre); *Smiley, The Night Alive,* (Lyric Theatre Belfast); *At The Ford* (Dublin Theatre Festival); *Luck Just Kissed you Hello,* (Mick Lally Theatre, Galway International Arts Festival).

Film/Television work: *The Second Violinist, The Last Hotel* (Landmark Productions); *The Date,* (Blinder Films); *Little Women,* (PBS/Ardmore Studios); *Rebellion,* (RTE); *A Dangerous Fortune,* (Octagon films): *We have always lived in the Castle* (Further Films 2016).

Hans Christian Andersen's

THE RED SHOES

in a new version by
Nancy Harris

Acknowledgements

My deepest gratitude to Selina Cartmell – for everything to do with this extraordinary journey into the dark heart of fairytales.

I would also like to thank the actors, dancers and creative team who took part in the workshop of the first draft of this play at the Gate in June 2017. Their commitment and creativity were integral to the development of this piece. They were: Marion O'Dwyer, Owen Roe, Robbie O'Connor, Barbara Brennan, Barry O'Connor, Leah Minto, Liv O'Donoghue, Ailish Maher, Ryan O'Neill, Monica Frawley, Paul Keoghan, Liz Roche and Marc Teitler.

I would also like to thank Rochelle Stevens and my family – Anne, Eoghan Connie, Mungo, Mirkev, Sophs and Kwasi.

N.H.

For Kev

Characters

KAREN, *an orphan, sixteen*

THE NUGENTS, *her adoptive family*
MARIELLA NUGENT, *housewife and aspiring member of the prestigious Save the Orphans Foundation*
BOB NUGENT, *Mariella's husband, property developer and aspiring casino owner*
CLIVE NUGENT, *their son, an executioner, twelve to seventeen*

SYLVESTOR, *narrator, shoemaker, mercurial*
MAGS, *country woman and fairy godmother of sorts. But she does not turn pumpkins into carriages*
PRIEST, *a priest, possibly played by the same actor as Sylvestor*
PRINCE, *Karen's love interest, seventeen*

And MOURNERS, GUESTS, SHADOWS, VOICES, *to be played by the ensemble of actors, dancers and musicians*

This text went to press before the end of rehearsals and so may differ slightly from the play as performed.

Note on Play

Multiple locations are suggested but the intention is that scenes move as fluidly as possible from one into the next. Any props mentioned that are not central to the action are merely suggestions, not necessities.

Likewise, any dance or movement suggested in the script should be seen as merely a starting point for further invention and can be developed or discarded as needed.

( ) indicate a line or a word that isn't necessarily spoken but conveyed in a thought

– at the end of sentence indicates an interruption

/ indicates an overlap in dialogue

… indicates an unfinished or unarticulated thought

– mid-sentence indicates a very brief pause or a beat where a thought is being clarified

6

Prologue

Darkness.

Then –

A single light as SYLVESTOR *appears and steps onto the stage.*

Some sort of beautiful red curtain behind him.

He looks at us.

He clears his throat.

He smiles.

He waits.

SYLVESTOR. Once Upon a Time.

   Beat.

   Happily Ever After.

   Beat.

   Once Upon a Time

   Happily Ever After.

   He looks at us again.

   Oh come on.

   You know the drill.

   You came here with some time to kill

   To hear a story you half-know

   About handsome princes

   Girls who clean

   While they're enslaved by wicked queens.

   Pumpkins turn to carriages? A gingerbread house?

   In a Disney version there's a talking mouse

Yeah?

He looks at us.

Smiles.

We know them as well as we know ourselves

Cos we've got the books up on our shelves

Where they sit – just like old friends.

And everything turns out alright in the end.

…Doesn't it?

The stage grows darker.

Doesn't it?

Handsome princes?

Fabulous balls?

He looks at us, ominous.

Do we know ourselves at all?

Or are we like forests – dark and deep?

Full of secrets we'd like to keep.

And is this real life –

or are we asleep?

Sharing the same dark dream.

He laughs, throwing it off.

Enough with all that.

Let's just start

I know that you all know this part

Once Upon a Time…

Does he open the curtain?

The ENSEMBLE *are behind it – dressed as* MOURNERS.

…Happily Ever After?

We Shall See.

You'll Stay there

But Follow me…

SYLVESTOR *steps in to join the* ENSEMBLE.

Oh – and if you're looking for fairies

Don't hold your breath

Cos this little fairytale

Starts with a death.

The MOURNERS *part, and reveal a simple wooden coffin.*

A country funeral.

Music.

The MOURNERS *sit on one side of the coffin and wait. Hawkish.*

When they talk, each one takes a different sentence, sometimes talking over each other – a chorus of sorts.

KAREN *enters the church, simply dressed, grief-stricken.*

The MOURNERS *watch her, vulture-like, as she walks by.*

She takes a seat in a chair in front of the coffin and looks at it, desolate.

The MOURNERS *whisper as though she isn't there.*

MOURNER 1 (*disapproving*). So that's what she wears to her mother's funeral? /

MOURNER 2. Priest wouldn't have known where to look.

MOURNER 1 *tuts.*

MOURNER 3. Suppose her mother picked that dress and all /

MOURNER 4. Sure think of what she used to wear herself /

MOURNER 5. With half the men in town knocking on her door.

Stifled sniggers.

They remember where they are and correct themselves.

MOURNERS/ALL (*a kind of keening*). God rest her soul.

KAREN *gets up and moves towards the coffin – reaching out to touch it.*

The MOURNERS *watch her, hawkish.*

A sense they are trying to publically out-mourn her.

She sits back down, quickly.

MOURNER 6. O'course they dressed differently where her mother was from /

MOURNER 7. It's hot there /

MOURNER 8. Probably don't need as many clothes.

MOURNER 4. Any.

They snigger again.

MOURNERS/ALL. God rest her soul.

KAREN *gets up to move towards the coffin again.*

They study KAREN *again, as though she's some sort of curious specimen.*

She sits back down again, self-conscious.

MOURNER 2. Say she hasn't cried.

MOURNER 1. Not so much as one tear.

MOURNER 3. Very unnatural /

MOURNERS 5. *Most* unnatural /

MOURNER 3. Imagine going to your own mother's funeral and letting people see you *not* crying.

MOURNER 1 *tuts.*

MOURNER 5. Doesn't talk either.

MOURNER 6. No? /

MOURNER 7. Not since she found the poor woman lying cold.

MOURNER 8. What sort of girl is she at all?

MOURNER 1. Different /

MOURNER 2. Just like the mother.

They lean forward and talk to KAREN – *as though she doesn't speak English.*

MOURNER 5. We cleaned the house for you!

KAREN *stares at them, not answering.*

MOURNER 1. You're welcome!

MOURNER 4. Place was in a right state /

MOURNER 1. Don't suppose your mother was doing much cleaning, the way her mind was at.

KAREN *doesn't respond.*

The MOURNERS *look at one another, knowing.*

MOURNER 5. We went through her things /

MOURNER 6. Very /

MOURNER 7. Carefully.

MOURNER 8. Threw out the rubbish.

MOURNER 7. There was plenty of that.

One of the MOURNERS *has on a string of pearls, another a pair of red gloves.*

They finger them, pleased.

MOURNER 2. …There *were* a few bits we kept for ourselves /

MOURNER 7. Only right /

MOURNER 8. Not like she can take them with her now.

They laugh.

MOURNERS. God rest her soul

KAREN *suddenly makes a dash to snatch the pearls.*

The MOURNERS *snatch them away.*

MOURNER 1 (*outrage*). Vanity is a sin, young lady.

MOURNER 3. Your mother learned that the hard way when she had you.

MOURNER 2. When you carry on like she did, you get what's coming to you.

MOURNER 4. Dancing and singing.

MOURNER 5. And putting it about.

MOURNER 6. Wasn't right in the head.

KAREN *draws back, hurt.*

The MOURNERS *lean forward sinister, threatening.*

MOURNER 7. Things won't be like they were, you know /

MOURNER 8. Not where you're going.

MOURNER 3. Does she know where she's going?

KAREN *shakes her head, worried.*

They smile, sinister.

MOURNER 2. Out of sight, out of mind /

MOURNER 4. Priest'll come for you in the morning. He'll explain.

MOURNER 5. How old is she now?

MOURNER 6. Sixteen they say /

MOURNER 7. Sixteen's a dangerous age /

MOURNER 8. And she's got sin running through her veins.

They look at her.

MOURNER 5. You should pack your things. You won't be back.

MOURNER 1. Take something to remember your mother.

KAREN *looks around. The room is bare.*

She looks back at the MOURNERS, *then goes towards them reaching for the pearls again.*

The MOURNER *slaps her hand away.*

MOURNER 1. Ungrateful girl!

MOURNER 5. She'll soon pay.

MOURNER 6. If I were you, young lady –

MOURNER 7. I'd get on my knees and pray.

They walk off into the darkness.

KAREN is left alone in the dark, empty room.

She looks at the coffin.

Faint strains of music can be heard somewhere, off.

She moves around the coffin, touching it, stroking it – her grief evident in her movement.

She climbs on top of the coffin.

On the coffin lid, she does a beautiful, mournful, balletic dance.

She looks down and puts her hand on the wood – as though she sees something.

Then… as if by some kind of strange magic, KAREN begins to pull a beautiful red scarf out through the coffin lid. She pulls and pulls it.

She smells the scarf and holds it to her face. It smells of her mother.

She cradles it, then wraps it around her neck.

Then she lies down on the coffin and holds it, as if trying to embrace her mother.

She stays like that and falls asleep.

The evening turns to darkness turns to…

ACT ONE

One

Shafts of morning light fall on the sleeping KAREN.

The coffin is has become a table or is now gone.

And the PRIEST *is standing over her.*

PRIEST.…Karen? Karen, wake up now.

    KAREN *wakes, disorientated, as the* PRIEST *pulls her up.*

    On your feet, there's a good girl. Were you praying all night?

    KAREN *nods.*

    Well, the Lord in his beneficence has heard you.

    KAREN *looks at him, confused.*

    There's been a change of plan – you're not going where you thought you were going.

    He starts to move around her. Vigorously brushing her clothes.

    Now, stand up straight and make yourself presentable. None of this slouching. Dry those red eyes. You want to make a good impression, don't you. Course you do. And there's no time to waste – they could be here literally any –

    And suddenly the door busts open and the NUGENTS – BOB *and* MARIELLA, *wearing fur – enter the room, talking. They look around, disdainful.*

MARIELLA. I don't believe it, Bob, do you believe it /

BOB. It's on the map /

MARIELLA. But it's so small and dark and –

    She sniffs.

    What *is* that smell?

BOB. I think they call it the countryside.

The PRIEST *rushes towards them –*

PRIEST. Mr and Mrs Nugent! Welcome. Welcome. You found us alright?

MARIELLA. Just about. We drove through the town at least twice.

BOB (*gruff*). If you could call it a town.

MARIELLA. Well, exactly.

BOB. No shops.

MARIELLA. No boutiques.

BOB. Not even a cashpoint.

MARIELLA. I mean what do people *do* here all day –

MARIELLA *sees* KAREN *and gasps*.

Oh my God is that our orphan?

PRIEST. It certainly is. Mariella, this is Karen. Karen, this is Bob and Mariella Nugent. They drove from Dublin this morning especially.

The PRIEST *pushes* KAREN *towards them*.

Mrs Nugent is a member of the prestigious Save the Orphans Foundation.

BOB *laughs*.

BOB. Ha! Where did you hear that?

MARIELLA *looks at* BOB, *a touch hurt*.

MARIELLA. Bob. Well, no I'm not a member – just yet, Father. Though very nearly – I have an application in for the board. I'm told I'm in with a very good chance.

She looks at KAREN.

You do know the prestigious Save the Orphans Foundation, don't you, dear?

KAREN *shakes her head*.

BOB. She must have seen them on the news.

PRIEST. Everybody who's anybody is a member.

KAREN *looks at them blank, shakes her head.*

MARIELLA. Well… I s'pose it is remote here.

PRIEST. Bob and Mariella have some *very* good news for you, Karen. They might be able to offer you a home.

KAREN *looks at them, surprised.*

MARIELLA. Well, we *were* hoping for something smaller.

PRIEST. Oh, she's not as tall as she looks, are you, Karen?

KAREN *shakes her head and instinctively hunches.*

MARIELLA. Cos the small ones are quiet and keep to themselves.

PRIEST. Oh she's very quiet, aren't you, Karen?

KAREN *nods quickly, silently.*

(*Aside*.) Hasn't said a word since her mother passed, in fact.

MARIELLA.…Does she eat?

PRIEST. Oh anything. Everything. And barely at all. She's like a little bird.

BOB. And she's not unstable?

PRIEST. (*with a laugh*) No –

BOB. Cos some of these orphans – with their backgrounds and history…

PRIEST. Karen's a very steady girl. Despite the situation with her – mother

MARIELLA/BOB. Terrible. Terrible. /

PRIEST. Karen has her head very much screwed on.

The PRIEST *knocks on* KAREN's *head.*

Haven't you, Karen?

KAREN *nods*.

MARIELLA *assesses her closely.*

MARIELLA. Hmmn.

KAREN *smiles, trying to be pleasing.*

…What do you think, Bob?

BOB*'s looking at his phone, checking emails.*

BOB. About what?

MARIELLA. About the orphan. Should we take her?

BOB. This is your thing, Mariella. Nothing to do with me.

MARIELLA. He was your second cousin.

BOB. Three times removed.

MARIELLA (*to the* PRIEST). Bob knew her father as
    I mentioned.

KAREN *looks up, sharp, intrigued.*

Oh that's got her interested. Ears practically pricking up.

PRIEST. Well, no one here knows much about Karen's father.
    Her mother never talked about him, understandably. I'm sure
    she's very keen to hear what he was like, aren't you, Karen?

KAREN *nods and goes to* BOB*, looking at him intensely.*

…What *was* he like?

BOB*, unused to teenage girls, backs away.*

BOB. Uh well… Mariella, the orphan is staring at me.

MARIELLA (*to* KAREN). Oh he was a terrible drinker, your
    father. Drank himself into an early grave. Liver as green as
    an olive in the end by all accounts.

BOB. Eyes as black as… onions.

This doesn't quite have the right descriptive effect.

MARIELLA. Most disturbing. So when we heard the news about
    your poor mother, God rest her soul, we said we can't just
    stand idle and do nothing to help. We must offer the girl some
    support… Of course we *were* hoping you'd be smaller…

PRIEST (*with a laugh*). Just put her in a corner, you won't know she's there.

KAREN *nods*.

MARIELLA *studies* KAREN, *considering*.

MARIELLA. I do like her sorrow around the eyes…

PRIEST. And she's sixteen now. Sure in one or two years she'll be off on her own –

MARIELLA. You're right. You know what – you're right. I think we'll take her!

BOB. So we're done?

MARIELLA (*to* KAREN). Where are her things?

PRIEST. Oh she barely has any. These are all her worldly goods.

The PRIEST *picks up a small simple suitcase.*

MARIELLA. A simple suitcase. (*Thrilled.*) The tragedy.

MARIELLA *takes it.*

Thank you for all your help, Father. We so appreciate it. Bob…

BOB *reaches into his pocket for a chequebook.*

BOB. What do we owe you, Father?

PRIEST. Oh for goodness' sake, she's hardly for sale. I'm just glad she's going to a loving home.

BOB. Oh grand so –

BOB *starts to put the chequebook away. The* PRIEST *panics.*

PRIEST. – though a small donation is always appreciated…

BOB. Of course.

BOB *takes the chequebook back out, starts to write.*

As MARIELLA *grips* KAREN*'s hand, leads her outside.*

MARIELLA. You come with me, love, we're just parked outside. See that gold convertible out by the gate.

KAREN *looks outside and stops, amazed.*

Oh, Bob, would you look at her face. Only this morning she thought she was going to a children's home and now – she thinks she's in a fairytale – (*To* KAREN.) Bet you can't believe your luck.

BOB *tears out the cheque and hands it to the* PRIEST.

PRIEST. Bless you, Mr Nugent.

BOB. Yeah, thanks.

Two

Music. Fairytale-like.

The ENSEMBLE *might arrive and create the Nugents' house in Dublin. A suggestion of opulence. White interiors. Orchids, tables, flowers…*

Around the room, various stuffed taxidermy animals – crows, otters, hares – both strange and terrifying.

MARIELLA *enters with* KAREN, *who stares around in wonder. She's never been anywhere like this.*

MARIELLA. Here we are – home sweet home. Now don't be alarmed by the class and style, dear. That's just a chandelier. You've probably seen those in magazines.

KAREN *goes to sit down on one of the chairs.* MARIELLA *stops her.*

Oh no, not there, dear. It was just dry-cleaned. We'll get you washed and dressed and scrubbed up later, then you can sit anywhere you like.

KAREN *stands awkward, as* MARIELLA *moves around.*

Now, where is Clive, he'll be dying to – Clive! CLIVE!

A young boy, CLIVE, *walks on carrying the bloodied carcass of a dead cat. The blood drips along the floor…*

CLIVE. Look what I just got!

He holds up the cat.

MARIELLA. Clive – oh Jesus, it's the Morrisons' cat. What have you done to him?

CLIVE. Nothing. He was like this on the road.

MARIELLA. He must've gotten himself run over. Quick, Clive, put him back before the neighbours find out!

CLIVE. I want to stuff him.

MARIELLA. Absolutely not.

CLIVE. Why?

MARIELLA. Because – he's a family pet.

CLIVE. He's the same as all the others.

MARIELLA. You found the others in the forest. They didn't have owners.

She gestures to the animals.

(*To* KAREN.) Clive made all of these himself. He's always in the forest, bringing things back. He's wonderfully artistic, isn't he, Bob?

BOB *comes in with* KAREN*'s suitcase.*

BOB. That's what we call it, yeah.

MARIELLA. He has his own studio out in the back. With all his special… implements.

CLIVE. I'm cutting up the cat.

She stops him.

MARIELLA. No you're not.

BOB. I've to make a few calls.

She stops him too.

MARIELLA. No you don't. You can both wait here. We've got ourselves a guest.

CLIVE. Is that the orphan?

MARIELLA. Her name's Karen, yes.

A beat as CLIVE *sizes her up.*

CLIVE. …I don't like her.

MARIELLA. She's just lost her mother, Clive, try to be nice.

He holds up the carcass.

CLIVE (*to* KAREN). Do you want to watch me cut up a cat?

KAREN *steps back and shakes her head, horrified.*

An old lady, MAGS, *enters with a mop and bucket. Her eyesight isn't good. She points to the floor.*

MAGS. Someone's gone and spilled something on the tiles…

MARIELLA. Ah, wonderful. Mags is here.

MAGS. I only mopped the place this morning. Soon as one bit's done, another appears…

She squints at the blood.

…What is it?

Then leans down, puts her finger in the blood and tastes it.

Chocolate?

She makes a face.

S'pose I'll have to clean it up.

MARIELLA. Just leave it for now and come and meet Karen – she's the orphan we've been telling you about. (*To* KAREN.) Mags is our housekeeper – been with us for years. Blind as a bat, but she means well.

MAGS *comes close and starts to feel* KAREN *with her hands.*

MAGS. She's big for an orphan.

MARIELLA. Well, we'd hoped for something smaller.

MAGS *feels around* KAREN's *face.*

MAGS. …She's pretty.

MARIELLA *studies* KAREN – *a flicker of jealousy.*

MARIELLA. In certain kinds of light.

MARIELLA *glances at* BOB, *but he's engrossed on his phone.*

She has a lovely bit of sorrow around the eyes.

MAGS *takes* KAREN*'s hand.*

MAGS. To lose your mother is a terrible thing. And so close to Christmas.

MARIELLA. Desperate, desperate. Now where is my…

MAGS (*genuine*). I'm very sorry for your loss. I'm sure Mr and Mrs Nugent will – try to take good care of you.

KAREN *looks at her, moved. It's the first time anyone has said it to her.*

MARIELLA. Bob and I just like to give back. Though as I always say, what's the point of giving if no one sees you give? Which is where we got the idea of having an orphan of our own. It was just blind luck we had one in the family.

MARIELLA *looks at* BOB, *a touch desperate.*

I mean the Save the Orphans Foundation can't ignore that, can they, Bob? They'll have to take us seriously now!

BOB. I'm on my knees praying for it.

MARIELLA *laughs, shrill.*

MARIELLA. That's his sense of humour. (*To* KAREN *explaining.*) Bob's a builder –

BOB. Purveyor of properties.

MARIELLA. Best in the country.

BOB. I buy land, I beautify it – with luxury apartments, complexes and the like – and I sell it. For a small profit.

He offers KAREN *his card.*

MARIELLA. He has very grand plans for the forest, haven't you, Bob?

BOB (*proud*). Casino. Best this country's ever seen. Twelve storeys high. Two football pitches wide. Everything included. Black Jack, roulette, a stage for the magicians.

MARIELLA. Bob loves his bit of magic.

BOB. Here – I learned a new trick. Want to see?

MARIELLA. Of course she doesn't.

BOB *ignores her, goes into performance mode*.

BOB. Ladies and gentlemen, roll up roll up –

MARIELLA (*firm*). Not now, Bob.

She turns to KAREN.

Would you listen to us wittering on. We want to hear about *you*, Karen, don't we?

BOB. I'm happy to wait.

MARIELLA. No no, everyone sit down and listen to Karen. She's going to tell us all about herself.

BOB *and* CLIVE *sit*.

MAGS *leans on her mop*.

They all look at KAREN *expectantly*.

KAREN *stands awkwardly, unsure of what to say*.

Anything at all now.

BOB. Thought the priest said she couldn't speak.

MARIELLA. Oh that's right – (*Irritated*.) The grief or something. How annoying –

CLIVE. Maybe we can ask her some questions? And she can nod or shake her head?

MARIELLA. Yes! Yes. Good idea. Why don't you go first, Clive?

CLIVE (*to* KAREN). Can I cut your finger off?

KAREN *steps back, shocked*.

MARIELLA. Clive! (*To* KAREN.) What's your favourite food?

BOB. Not a yes or no.

MARIELLA. Dammit /

CLIVE. What about your little toe?

BOB. How about hobbies? Any of those?

> KAREN *nods*.

MARIELLA. Hobbies, good… Now what hobbies? Painting?

> MARIELLA *mimes painting – like a game of charades*.

> KAREN *shakes her head*.

No… Singing?

> KAREN *shakes her head*.

…No.

CLIVE. Chopping things up?

> MAGS *joins in*.

MAGS. What about dancing? (*To* KAREN.) Most young people like that.

MARIELLA. Do you, Karen?

> KAREN *looks at* MAGS *and smiles enthusiastically*.

> MARIELLA *claps her hands excitedly*.

She does!

> KAREN *nods*.

(*Excited*.) Do you hear that, Bob, the orphan likes to dance.

BOB. Well, I heard you say it, she's a mute.

MARIELLA. Bob and I used love to dance. We learned the tango on our second wedding anniversary on a cruise around the Riviera. Remember that, Bob? You wouldn't know to look at him, but he's got very agile hips. Why did we stop?

BOB. We got old.

> MARIELLA *looks at him a little sadly*.

> MAGS *looks at* KAREN.

MAGS. What sort of dancing does she do?

MARIELLA. Well, we don't know, do we. Maybe she'll show us a bit. (*To* KAREN.) Would you, Karen? Show us?

KAREN *steps back, shy. Shakes her head.*

Just one or two steps.

KAREN *shakes her head more fervently.*

MAGS. Ah leave her be. She's only just got here, the poor cratur.

MARIELLA. No no come on. There's no need to be embarrassed. We're all family here now. And you wouldn't want to upset your new family on your first day in their house, when they've been so good to you and taken you in, and treated you as one of their own – would you now, Karen?

Beat.

KAREN *tentatively shakes her head.*

Course you wouldn't.

MARIELLA *pulls* KAREN *into the centre of the room.*

So you stand there in the middle of the room where we all can see you – there's a good girl. And we'll sit here and watch you dance.

They all stare at KAREN.

KAREN *looks back, anxious.*

Whenever you're ready.

KAREN *knows she has no choice.*

She takes a nervous breath – every fibre of her being doesn't want to do this.

Then without music or anything, she self-consciously begins to dance – moving her hands, her legs, her body a little wildly. Maybe she bangs into some furniture?

The NUGENTS *watch her with curiosity and growing discomfort.*

Whatever they were expecting, it wasn't that.

After thirty seconds or so she stops.

The NUGENTS *stare at her.*

Suddenly BOB, MARIELLA *and* CLIVE *burst out laughing.*

KAREN *steps back, hurt.*

Well… /

CLIVE. What the hell was that?

MARIELLA. I've absolutely no idea.

BOB. If that's what they're calling dancing these days, I'm
a bleedin' ballerina.

MARIELLA *wipes away a tear of laughter.*

MARIELLA. Oh, Bob, stop.

MAGS *looks at* KAREN, *who is clearly hurt.*

MAGS. Well, her mother wasn't from here, isn't that what you
said? Maybe that's called dancing where she was from…

MARIELLA *gathers herself.*

MARIELLA. You're right, Mags, you're right. Foreigners have
a different way of doing things.

BOB. Cos it's not how we do it round here.

MARIELLA. No! Certainly not.

They stifle laughs again.

KAREN *shrinks back, mortified.*

Did you say that your mother also made you that dress?

KAREN *nods.*

Poor woman with her tormented mind.

KAREN *stands awkwardly, feeling like a fool.*

Well, don't you worry, Karen, you've come to the right place.
Mags and I will have you fixed up and looking normal in no
time. It's not who you are, it's who you know, as I always say.
Don't I, Mags?

She looks at MAGS.

MAGS. You do, Mrs Nugent. You do.

MARIELLA. Come along with us, dear. This way, this way –

MAGS *and* MARIELLA *take* KAREN *by the arms and lead her off.*

CLIVE *watches them go.*

CLIVE....How long's she staying for?

BOB. That's up to your mother.

CLIVE *looks at* BOB, *who's on his phone, distracted.*

CLIVE. Are you really building a casino in the forest?

BOB. If you build it, they will come…

BOB *laughs to himself.*

CLIVE *rolls his eyes.*

(*Re: his emails*.) Just need to sort out this planning permission first.

CLIVE. I like it as it is.

BOB. You'll like it better when there's waterslides. Trust me.

CLIVE *looks at the carcass of the cat.*

CLIVE. Can I gut and stuff the Morrisons' cat?

BOB (*distracted, not looking up*). What did your mother say?

CLIVE. She said it's fine.

BOB (*distracted*). Fine.

CLIVE. Cool!

CLIVE *rushes off with the cat.*

BOB. Here – want to see my new trick? It's a good one.

BOB *comes to the front of the stage, ceremoniously rolling up his sleeves. He takes out his handkerchief.*

Ladies and gentleman, sit back and marvel as I, Bob Nugent, an ordinary man, take this, an ordinary telephone –

He holds up his iPhone for us to see.

– and make it vanish. Into thin air.

He takes out his handkerchief, covers the phone, waves his hand ceremoniously over it –

– by the power of magic and mayhem and madness – on the count of one, two...

He looks around, realises CLIVE *has gone.*

Ah, is no one watching?... (*Calling.*) Clive?... That's just cruel.

He puts the phone back into his pocket, annoyed, then remembers.

Wait. Which cat?

BOB *rushes offstage after* CLIVE.

Three

The ENSEMBLE *enter either side with clothes rails full of extravagant pieces.*

A mirror, huge and magnificent, is placed in the middle of the room.

KAREN *is led in by* MARIELLA, MAGS *following.*

MARIELLA. Now – this is my dressing room. Never to be entered without my permission, understand?

KAREN *nods.*

Some of these pieces are worth more than this house.

MARIELLA *stands in front of the huge mirror and smiles.*

Mirror mirror, on the wall. Keep my complexion smooth and my waistline small...

She laughs.

Just my little joke. My waistline's always small. Bob and I bought this mirror on a business trip. Back when he used to take me with him… it talks, you know.

KAREN *looks at her, surprised.*

You just have to ask it a question. Look.

MARIELLA *stands in front of the mirror.*

Does a little twirl.

(*To the mirror.*) Mirror mirror, on the wall, how do I look today?

MIRROR (*cheerfully robotic voice*). You look great today – Mariella!

KAREN *smiles, pleased.*

MARIELLA. It's an affirmation mirror. Builds self-confidence. It's even got a memory.

She twirls again.

Mirror mirror, on the wall – how did I look yesterday?

MIRROR. You looked great yesterday – Mariella!

MARIELLA. Mags, you try it.

MAGS*, who is sorting out clothes rails, looks up.*

MAGS. Oh no, I've no truck with that thing.

MARIELLA. It's just a bit of fun!

MAGS. I can't abide its voice.

MARIELLA. Come on, Mags. For the orphan.

MAGS. Oh for goodness' sake.

MAGS *sighs. Goes to the mirror. Does a perfunctory twirl.*

…Mirror mirror, on the wall, how do I look today?

MIRROR. You look great today – Mags!

MAGS *shrugs it off.*

MAGS. Always says the same bleedin' thing. (*To* KAREN.) You try.

KAREN goes to the mirror, excited.

Does a happy little twirl.

Mirror mirror, on the wall, how does Karen look today?

Beat.

MIRROR. You're beautiful, Karen.

KAREN stops, surprised.

You're beautiful. Inside and out.

A shocked beat. MAGS *looks at* MARIELLA.

MAGS. Did you change the recording on it or something?

MARIELLA looks at KAREN *with cold surprise.*

MARIELLA. No.

MAGS. Never heard it say that before.

MARIELLA (*quickly*). Must be broken. You know what these old things are like.

She regards KAREN, *suspicious.*

Of course, vanity is a sin… and people who spend time admiring their own reflections usually meet very unhappy ends. Don't they, Mags?

MAGS. Well, I wouldn't say –

MARIELLA yanks KAREN *towards the clothes rails.*

MARIELLA. Come on, let's get you dressed. There's sure to be something much more sensible in here.

MAGS *and* MARIELLA *start to root through the clothes rails.*

MAGS *holds a pretty dress up to* KAREN.

MAGS. What about this? Feels nice and frilly.

KAREN smiles, liking it.

MARIELLA *shakes her head.*

MARIELLA. Too fussy.

She discards it.

MAGS *holds another pretty dress up to* KAREN.

MAGS. Or this? With the little sequins.

KAREN *smiles.*

MARIELLA. Too smart.

MARIELLA *discards it.*

KAREN *picks up a third pretty dress – holds it to herself and smiles hopefully at* MARIELLA.

MARIELLA *snatches the dress off her –*

Absolutely not. Where do you think you're off to – a ball!

She throws it on the floor and hands KAREN *another one.*

This is the one!

– it looks like a large, shapeless black sack. She holds it up to KAREN.

Oh yes, this will look great on you! Won't it, Mags –

MAGS *feels it, makes a face.*

MAGS. Feels a bit –

MARIELLA (*cutting her off*). Trust me, I have a good eye. Before I met Bob I was senior manager at a very exclusive department store. Course, I gave it up just after the wedding. No sense in an important man being married to a shop girl, is there.

She laughs, shrill.

Try it on, try it on.

KAREN *hesitates, self-conscious.*

Now don't be silly – we're all girls here. Mags, you help.

MAGS. Come here, love.

MAGS *blindly tries to help* KAREN *undress*.

MARIELLA *starts to sift through the rails*.

MARIELLA. We're having a dinner here on Friday – in your honour, Karen.

MAGS. Do you hear that, Karen? A party for you.

KAREN *smiles*.

MARIELLA. I'll have to look fabulous. The chairwoman of the Save the Orphans Foundation will be coming. It's one thing saving orphans in the abstract, but inviting one into your very own home… I mean if that doesn't get their attention…

Another shrill laugh.

MAGS. And Karen'll need to look her best too.

MARIELLA. But like an orphan, yes.

KAREN *steps out in the dress. It hangs on her long and drab*.

Oh. Stunning! It really accentuates your better features… do you like it?

KAREN *pulls at the loose fabric, deflated. She clearly doesn't*.

It's a vast improvement on what you had. Except for the shoes – they're grotesque. We'll have those burned.

MAGS. Burned! What about the charity shop?

MARIELLA. And inflict them on someone else?

KAREN *takes off her shoes*. MARIELLA *looks at* KAREN'*s feet and gasps*.

Oh dear God – look at her toes. They're all red and swollen.

MAGS *touches* KAREN'*s feet*.

MAGS. Must have been too small for her – poor thing.

MARIELLA *grimaces, unsympathetic*.

She pulls out a large pair of men's brown shoes.

MARIELLA (*to* KAREN). Here put these on for now. They're Bob's old ones but you've got big feet.

As MARIELLA *holds some dresses up to herself* KAREN *reluctantly puts on the shoes.*

They are huge and ridiculous on her.

As KAREN *clumps around in them,* MAGS *squints.*

MAGS. Don't sound too good.

MARIELLA. Just a little loose. She'll get used to them.

KAREN *stumbles in them.*

MAGS.…Maybe you should take her to that shoemaker. I heard he's back in town.

MARIELLA (*gasps*). Sylvestor! Since when?

MAGS. Since a few days ago they say. You know what he's like with his pop-up shop. One day he's here, next he's gone… Do you know about Sylvestor, Karen?

KAREN *shakes her head.*

MARIELLA. Of course she doesn't – she's from the country.

MAGS *comes close to* KAREN.

MAGS. Say he's the greatest shoemaker in the world.

MARIELLA. A wizard where feet are concerned /

MAGS. Travels all over. Brazil, Shanghai /

MARIELLA. Waiting list as long as my arm.

MAGS. Made me these boots – ten years ago now. Never bought a new pair since… Not a hole, not a scratch.

MARIELLA. And of course he made these.

MAGS (*knowing*). Oh yes… wait'll you see these.

MARIELLA *with great flourish pulls down a beautiful painted box.*

MARIELLA. Hand-crafted to order. From Mulberry silk. There's not another pair like them in the world… Want to look?

KAREN *nods eagerly.*

MARIELLA *opens the lid.* KAREN *looks inside.*

A light from whatever magical thing is in there shines out on KAREN*'s face.*

She smiles in wonder. MARIELLA *points.*

Those are real rose petals there by the heel and that's a real live butterfly on the toe. See it flap its little wings.

KAREN*, mesmerised, reaches in to touch it.*

MARIELLA *slams the lid shut on her fingers.*

No touching!

KAREN *is stunned.*

I only wear them on very special occasions.

MARIELLA *studies* KAREN.

Taking her to Sylvestor seems a bit extravagant.

MAGS. But if her feet are as bad as you say…

MARIELLA. But what does she need a special pair of shoes for – we can get her a normal pair from a shop.

KAREN *is visibly deflated.*

We don't want her getting notions.

MAGS *glances at* KAREN*, sympathetic. An idea occurring.*

MAGS.…You're right, Mrs Nugent. It was a silly idea.

MARIELLA *nods.*

MARIELLA. Yes.

MAGS.…I was only thinking of this dinner on Friday with the Save the Orphans Foundation. And how impressed all those important, glamorous people would be by your generosity in buying a poor orphan with no belongings of her own, a pair of properly well-made shoes.

MARIELLA *turns, suddenly intrigued.*

MAGS *waves it away.*

But don't listen to me, it's a foolish thought.

MARIELLA. Well, hang on –

MAGS. No, no it's ridiculous, I wasn't thinking –

MARIELLA. Though we don't want people saying we're neglecting her.

MAGS. Sure you can buy an ordinary pair of shoes in town.

MARIELLA. That's true.

MAGS. Just cos it might impress a committee –

MARIELLA. Well, that's true too.

MAGS. But who cares about them?

MARIELLA. Well, I do /

MAGS. They're only rich people. Why spend good money on an orphan when you can save that very same money for yourself.

MARIELLA *looks at* KAREN.

MARIELLA. Well, it's important that she's comfortable.

MAGS. Most people wouldn't bother.

MARIELLA. Well, I'm not most people –

MAGS. Most people would just put her in front of the Foundation wearing any old pair of shoes at all.

MARIELLA. Well, I'm not most people! I'm Mariella Nugent. And no orphan of mine is going to be seen wandering around in an ordinary pair of shoes, when she can just as easily have a designer pair made specially. You're to take her to Sylvestor at once.

MAGS *nods, utterly aware of what she's done*.

MAGS. ...if you think it's a good idea.

MARIELLA. Wild horses couldn't change my mind!

MAGS *smiles to herself*.

MAGS. I'll phone him first thing in the morning.

KAREN, *who has been listening to this, suddenly lunges at* MARIELLA *and gives her a hug*.

MARIELLA *steps back, stunned*.

MARIELLA.…What's happening? Mags, she's…

KAREN *holds on*.

KAREN. Thank you, Mrs Nugent.

MARIELLA *steps back, shocked*.

MARIELLA. What!… Did she just… Did you just speak?

KAREN (*shy*). Yes, Mrs Nugent.

MARIELLA *gasps*.

MARIELLA. Would you listen to that, Mags. The orphan speaks. And perfect English too.

KAREN. You've been very kind to me.

MARIELLA *clasps her hands together.*

MARIELLA. Oh, how adorable. Yes I have, haven't I?

She pats KAREN*'s back.*

Make sure to mention that at the dinner.

KAREN *nods*.

Well, we mustn't get distracted by all this chatter. Let's get rid of these old things and run you a bath. By the looks of it you haven't washed in weeks. Mags, bring the bleach. We'll have a whole new Karen on our hands before we know it. You won't even recognise yourself. Come along.

MARIELLA *and* MAGS *gather up the clothes and go*.

KAREN *hangs back for a moment. She sees the red scarf on the floor where* MARIELLA *has dropped it*.

She picks it up and looks at it for a beat.

Then she quickly stuffs it into her dress, so MARIELLA *doesn't see.*

The ENSEMBLE *come on and begin to sing choral style (as they remove the props perhaps?).*

EMSEMBLE. Mirror mirror, on the wall

Keep my complexion smooth and my waistline small

Looking glass, what do you see

When I'm looking at you

I'm looking at me.

Show me what you have to hide

I can see the surface

But what's inside?

Four

The forest near the house. Evening.

It's growing dark and we hear the crowing of birds.

KAREN *is walking in* BOB*'s shoes, awkward and a little afraid. She looks around.*

She stumbles and we hear a crow squawking near her.

A shadow moves in the bushes.

KAREN *(afraid)*....hello?

> *Nothing.*

> ...is someone there?

> *She stops.*

> *Nothing.*

> *She looks around to make sure no one can see her.*

> *Then she takes off her clumpy men's shoes and socks.*

> *She takes out the red scarf and wraps it around herself.*

> *Then she closes her eyes and begins to dance.*

> *Music.*

> *Without an audience,* KAREN *is graceful, unselfconscious.*

> *Her dance is tentative but beautiful.*

*In the shadows, we see someone or something approach.
Dark, menacing.*

*Perhaps the shadow of an axe is thrown up on the wall
behind* KAREN.

It comes closer…

KAREN *keeps dancing, transported, oblivious… then
suddenly someone springs out at her.*

CLIVE. What are you doing?!

KAREN *jumps back, startled. Embarrassed.*

CLIVE *looks at her, something sinister in his eyes.*

The sense he knows she's somehow transgressed.

Does my mother know you're out here?

KAREN *shakes her head.*

She wouldn't like it. There are weirdos everywhere hiding
in trees…

He looks at her, sinister.

Forest is haunted. Everyone says. Back in the old days they
used to leave children out here. Children whose parents
didn't want them, children whose mothers shouldn't have
had them. (Children like you.) They'd take them out in the
dead of night, with no food and no blankets – knowing they
wouldn't find their way back. People say you can still hear
their ghosts crying.

KAREN.…I don't believe you.

CLIVE *makes a face.*

CLIVE. Get you. Talking now and everything.

KAREN *looks down, self-conscious.*

He comes towards her.

Have you ever seen a ghost before?

KAREN. Only my mother. I found her dead.

CLIVE. That's not a ghost, it's a corpse. I'm talking about real ghosts. I've seen spirits come through those trees…

He points.

KAREN. I wish my mother would come back and haunt me. Least then I could still see her face.

CLIVE. You're weird.

KAREN. What are you doing out here?

CLIVE. Hunting. The Morrisons wanted to bury their cat. Now I have to find something else to stuff.

He looks at her, a hint of menace.

He gestures to a block of wood with the axe.

…Want to put your head on that block?

KAREN *steps back, nervous. Shakes her head.*

What about your hand? Dare you.

KAREN. Why do you like chopping things up?

CLIVE. Why do you like dressing like that?

KAREN. Your mother gave me these.

CLIVE. Bet she did.

CLIVE *loses interest.*

He picks up a large piece of wood and puts it on the block. Then he holds the axe over it.

Chopping stuff's not as easy as it looks, you know. You have to get the angle exactly right. And the blade has to be sharp so it goes right through. Worst thing you can do is keep hacking away. Same for a human head – it's full of muscles and sinew and bone – it's hard to get a good clean slice. Takes an expert. When they chopped off Anne Boleyn's head, they brought the executioner over from France. Cos he was the best. He didn't even put her head on the block. Just lobbed it right off on her knees.

He brings the axe down hard and splits the wood.

KAREN *jumps*.

He looks at her and smiles.

…I'd be a good executioner.

He comes towards her.

No one'd even notice you're gone.

KAREN *steps back, afraid.*

KAREN…. Your mother would.

CLIVE. You think she likes you? Is that why you do everything she says? So she doesn't have a reason to send you back?

A beat.

KAREN *nods.*

You idiot. She doesn't need a reason. She could just wake up one morning and change her mind…

He picks up the axe, grinning.

I'm going home. Don't stay too long… When it gets dark the ghosts come out.

He sniggers.

KAREN *is left alone.*

She hears a rustling in the trees. The sound of the wind and a crow.

It scares her.

She quickly puts on the shoes and follows him…

Five

The forest near SYLVESTOR*'s pop-up shop.*

MAGS *is leading* KAREN *by the hand through the trees.*

MAGS. Come on, love, just through here…

> KAREN *stops, nervous.* MAGS *pulls her on.*

> I know it might seem like a bit of a strange place to have a shoe shop, but, well… I suppose Sylvestor *is* a bit strange. Pops up wherever you least expect him anyway. He can be a bit – temperamental. Creative types often are. But though he might show you lots of things you like the look of, just remember Mrs Nugent has given very clear instructions. And I've learned over the years that the best way to deal with Mrs Nugent is do exactly as she says. Keep your head down. Don't make a fuss. That way her gaze floats right over you and you can still keep a piece of who you are. Understand?

> KAREN *nods.*

> Good.

> KAREN *looks up and gasps.*

> *A prim, neatly dressed man has appeared beneath the trees, fastidiously polishing a pair of shoes. There's a small table in front of him.* SYLVESTOR, *the shoemaker.*

> KAREN *leans into* MAGS.

KAREN (*whispering*)….Is that him?

> MAGS *squints.*

MAGS. Sssh, keep your voice down. (*Whispering.*) He has very strict rules. We must wait till we're called. Our appointment's not till three.

> KAREN *waits.*

> SYLVESTOR *continues polishing as though they aren't there.*

> *After a while –*

KAREN. Does he even see us?

SYLVESTOR *puts down the shoes and looks right at*
KAREN.

SYLVESTOR. Oh I see you, Karen. Though others might not.

KAREN *is surprised. But he turns his gaze to* MAGS.

How are you, Margaret? It's been such a long time.

MAGS. Over a decade. Wasn't even sure you'd remember me.

SYLVESTOR. Remember? How could I forget.

He takes MAGS*'s hand and kisses it. She laughs, delighted.*

Mags, poor Mags with her poor tortured feet.

MAGS. Was I telling you about my corns last time?

SYLVESTOR. You don't have to tell me. I can hear them
screaming as we speak. Like children trapped in a house fire,
standing at the window shouting 'Let me out!'

MAGS. I've had a lifetime of suffering.

SYLVESTOR. Haven't we all? But you're here now – allow
yourself to slip into something more comfortable.

An armchair appears beside MAGS.

MAGS. Well, I shouldn't really when we're here on business…
though I have had this funny headache all day –

SYLVESTOR *nods sympathetic.*

SYLVESTOR. And why wouldn't you, with all you do for other
people. Sit back, relax, take the weight off.

He gives MAGS *a little push into the chair.*

MAGS. Oh.

SYLVESTOR. And tell me about this delightful creature
with you.

He casts a look at KAREN, *intrigued.*

MAGS. Well… this is Karen – she's the orphan Mrs Nugent's
just taken in.

SYLVESTOR *studies* KAREN.

SYLVESTOR. Orphan. Fascinating…

He smiles.

MAGS. Mrs Nugent sent us here because Karen needs a new pair of…

She yawns, her eyes get droopy.

…my goodness this chair's very comfortable…

SYLVESTOR. You were saying?

MAGS*'s head begins to loll back. She tries to fight it.*

MAGS. Yes I was saying… what was I saying? Well, Mrs Nugent is very particular and she… she… Oh dear I don't know what's come over me… I could almost… fall… as-lee–

MAGS *falls asleep.*

SYLVESTOR *creeps towards* MAGS. *Maybe opens one of her eyelids.*

SYLVESTOR. It appears she's nodded off.

He smiles.

Guess that leaves just you and me… Karen?

KAREN *nods, uncertain.*

Karen. A simple name that hides so much… Have we met before?

KAREN *shakes her head.*

He comes towards her, eyeing her intently.

You seem familiar… Strange.

KAREN *shifts, uneasy.*

He shakes it off.

Well, Karen. Tell me. What can I do for you?

KAREN *swallows – shy.*

KAREN. I just… need a pair of shoes.

SYLVESTOR. You just need a pair of shoes…

He laughs.

He stops.

He looks at her.

If only it were as straightforward as that.

People say the eyes are the windows to the soul.

But they're wrong.

It's the feet.

He steps out from behind the table.

For the first time we see he's wearing a pair of emerald-green stilettos that sparkle in the light. KAREN *stares at them in surprise.*

SYLVESTOR *grins, brings his finger to his lips and does a little twirl.*

Think of your feet.

What they know.

What they carry.

How they parry –

from Billy to Jack

from home to work and back

from the lies and deceits

and the daily defeats

humiliations, depravities

bruised egos

tooth cavities

Squeezed and abused

into ill-fitting shoes

Bunioned and calloused

Yet they give us our ballast.

They don't howl

they don't swear

they don't give in to despair

we hardly even notice that they're there

…Till they're not.

Our feet are really all we've got.

But do we treat them as we should?

With love and care and endless good?

No! We give them no respect –

We leave them swollen, bruised, wrecked

simply something to be fecked

into whatever high-street sandal comes along

Cheap and nasty

Made of plastic

You and I both know it's wrong

Because we'll miss them when they're gone

Believe you me…

He comes towards her, taking a piece of her hair in his fingers.

You brush your hair

You brush your teeth

But you don't think about your feet

the way they think about you.

…Don't they deserve more?

Don't they deserve better?

Don't they deserve real Italian leather?

Don't they deserve to be cloaked in feathers

To bring us high above the earth –

Where we can soar… (*Does he sing this?*)

No more crying

Now you're flying

Cos the feet

Oh the feet

…Have soles too.

He grins at her.

Beat.

What do you think? Poet or what?

KAREN *stares at him sort of mesmerised.*

MAGS *wakes up.*

MAGS. Oh Jesus I forgot! Mrs Nugent wrote us a note.

SYLVESTOR. A note?

MAGS. On a piece of paper. Now where did I…

As MAGS *rustles in her bag for a bit of paper,* SYLVESTOR *keeps his eyes locked on* KAREN, *studying her.*

MAGS *pulls the paper out.*

Ah yes here! Now I know you like to do things your own way, Sylvestor, but I really think for the girl's sake it's important that we listen to Mrs Nugent.

SYLVESTOR *yawns –*

SYLVESTOR. Sure we'll listen… doesn't mean we'll hear.

MAGS *glances at him uncertain, clears her throat.*

Maybe she pulls out an eyeglass or something and tries to read.

MAGS. Now let me just try to… Dear Shapemaker, Shape-shifter, Shoemaker!… makes more sense. (*To* KAREN.) Can you read that?

KAREN *reaches for it.*

SYLVESTOR *snatches it away. He reads.*

SYLVESTOR. Dear Shoemaker. Please find Karen a pair of shoes. They should be all of the following: plain, simple, modest, sensible even to the point of dull. They should not be any of the following: glamorous, attention-seeking, fabulous. We don't want to give her notions about herself, brackets – she's a just poor religious country girl after all – close brackets.

Brief beat as KAREN *digests.*

Then he reads the final line –

Something on the reasonable side if possible. Smiley face. Mariella Nugent.

He folds the paper and gives it to MAGS.

MAGS.... Would you have anything like that?

SYLVESTOR. We have everything the heart desires.

MAGS (*relieved*). Oh good.

He dives behind the work desk and pulls out an ugly, plain-black leather shoe.

SYLVESTOR. I believe something like this is what Mrs Nugent was describing...

He dumps it on the table.

(*To* KAREN.) Does your heart's desire look like this?

KAREN *hesitates. Clearly not.*

MAGS *steps in.*

MAGS. She just wants to make Mrs Nugent happy, don't you, Karen?

KAREN *nods.*

Making Mrs Nugent happy is something you must think about when you're under Mrs Nugent's roof. Don't get me wrong she's not a – terrible woman. She took me in when I needed work. And so she doesn't pay me handsomely for washing her linen and scrubbing her floors till my knees are red raw, but as she says herself – what do I need money for anyway? Wouldn't I only spend it if I had it?

SYLVESTOR *yawns again, turns to* MAGS.

SYLVESTOR. Perhaps you should have another little sleep.

MAGS. Huh?

He sprinkles some glitter or something on her head and MAGS *instantly conks out.*

KAREN (*shocked*). Mags!… What did you do to her?

KAREN *goes to* MAGS *and shakes her. She doesn't wake up.*

SYLVESTOR. Simply helped her succumb to her desire. Sure the poor woman's exhausted from a lifetime of toil – and tragedy. Leave her be.

He takes KAREN*'s hand.*

Let's talk about me. No, you! Let's talk about you.

He picks up the ugly leather shoe on the table.

Is this really your kind of shoe?

KAREN *hesitates, then nods.*

Sure?

KAREN *nods.*

He comes towards her, looking at her closely.

Cos I don't think that's quite true.

There's a hunger in you, Karen.

There's a passion.

I can see it in your eyes.

KAREN. It's sorrow… Mrs Nugent says.

SYLVESTOR. Why should you eat crumbs, Karen –

While the rest of them eat cake?

Why should you eat morsels

When you can have the whole damn boulangerie!

Suddenly the lights change – or the ENSEMBLE *appear –
and several glass cabinets filled with shoes of every colour
and description appear.*

They twinkle in the light – like different-coloured sweets.

KAREN *steps back. stunned.*

Isn't it fabulous?

It's here for the taking –

You can have any dish on this table

Whatever whets your poor deprived appetite

He picks up some shoes and begins to juggle them.

Something gold

Something purple

Something mink

Something turtle

Something bright

Something dark

Something made of oak tree bark

Smell that…

She smells the shoes.

KAREN. Wow.

He grabs something else.

SYLVESTOR. These I made from orange peel

That's the skin of an electric eel

Crocodile is so last Tuesday

But otter's all the rage.

KAREN*'s overwhelmed as he moves through the various
shoe shelves.*

Whatever you want

Take your pick

Just make sure to make it quick –

The old woman won't sleep forever, you know.

KAREN looks at him nervous.

KAREN. But Mrs Nugent…

SYLVESTOR. Mrs Nugent, Mrs Boo-gent!

He looks at us.

Does that work?

He shrugs it off.

I understand the hesitation, Karen. You just want to be the nice girl. Speak when you're spoken to, do as you're told. You don't want to cause trouble… or let anyone see the fire that rages beneath.

He pulls the long red scarf out from where KAREN*'s concealed it under her dress.*

…but I see it.

She snatches the scarf back.

And I know just – what you're looking for.

He points.

And suddenly KAREN *sees them.*

Maybe they drop from the ceiling. Or maybe they're spotlit, high up on a shelf.

The red shoes.

Sparkling and inviting. Utterly different from anything else.

KAREN *stares at them.*

Step a little closer…

Have a good look…

KAREN *slowly starts to move towards the shoes.*

Maybe she has to climb up to lift them down?

But when she has them, she takes them in her hands, staring at them like beautiful jewels.

And tell me they don't set your heart on fire.

KAREN. My mother… had a pair like these…

SYLVESTOR. Your mother?

Does he know something?

KAREN *keeps looking at them.*

KAREN. Red was her favourite colour… She used to dance in them. She was such a good dancer. Whenever she wore them, people stopped in the street and – stared.

SYLVESTOR.…I'll bet you'd like that, wouldn't you, Karen? To have people look at you like that?

She looks at him, then nods.

…Try them on.

We see the longing in KAREN.

But she shakes her head.

They're just a pair of shoes, Karen. They won't bite… unless you want them to.

KAREN. They're not what Mrs Nugent wants.

SYLVESTOR. Who cares what Mrs Nugent wants?

KAREN. I do.

SYLVESTOR. What about what you want?

Beat.

It's just you and me here, Karen. What's the harm in knowing if they'll fit?

He's having an effect on her.

Just for a minute.

KAREN. Well… maybe just for a minute… Before Mags wakes up.

SYLVESTOR. Now you're talking.

KAREN kicks off the clumpy men's ones and puts the red shoes on the ground.

A beat while she considers.

Then she quickly puts her feet inside them.

SYLVESTOR *gasps.*

Like they were made for you!

And instantly we see a difference in KAREN.

KAREN. They feel so…

SYLVESTOR. Different?

KAREN.…They don't squeeze or pinch my toes.

SYLVESTOR. Of course not.

She wiggles her feet.

KAREN. They sort of… tingle.

SYLVESTOR. Tingle?

KAREN. They make me want to…

And suddenly she moves, quick, lithe, dancing across the room.

She stops suddenly. Shocked.

What was that?

SYLVESTOR (*innocent*). What?

KAREN. They just moved.

She looks at her shoes confused.

SYLVESTOR. Did they? Well… you do like dancing. Don't you, Karen?

She looks up, sharp.

KAREN. How do you know that?

SYLVESTOR. Same way I know anything, my dear. I listen to the feet.

KAREN (*quickly*). Well, I don't any more.

SYLVESTOR. Why ever not?

KAREN. Cos... I'm no good.

Beat.

SYLVESTOR.... You – could be good, if you want to be...
the shoes can help. These shoes were made for dancing.

SYLVESTOR *kneels down, takes a shoe in his hand.*

For an Argentinian dancer, to be exact. One of the greats...
She ordered the fabric herself from a medicine man in Peru.
Said she wanted me to make her a second pair of feet.

KAREN *looks at the shoes.*

KAREN. So... why doesn't she have them?

SYLVESTOR. An accident. Terrible really, I don't like to talk
about it. Suffice it to say she's not dancing now.

He looks at KAREN *knowingly.*

I suppose passion has its price... Luckily the shoes found
their way back to me, though no one's had the courage to
buy them. Yet.

He runs his hands over KAREN*'s shoes. A spell?*

Pity... They're such pretty dancing shoes!

Something – a little bit of music.

KAREN *suddenly jolts and jerks.*

*And out of nowhere she jumps/moves – quick, agile – across
the room.*

She stops quickly, frightened, thrilled.

Looks at him.

KAREN. What's happening?

She moves again.

I don't understand...

She moves again.

SYLVESTOR. Oh, I think you do.

She moves again.

KAREN. I feel strange…

SYLVESTOR. You look fabulous. And the way you move…

KAREN *dances – easy, effortless.*

Doesn't it feel good?

Does SYLVESTOR *join her?*

Don't you feel happy?… Don't you feel a sudden sense of possibility? A sense that your troubles are drifting away…

KAREN. Yes…

SYLVESTOR.… You're free.

She moves again, vibrant.

KAREN. Yes.

SYLVESTOR. You don't care what anyone thinks.

KAREN. No.

SYLVESTOR. Say it.

KAREN. I don't care what anyone thinks.

She moves faster.

SYLVESTOR. Again.

KAREN. I don't care what anyone thinks.

SYLVESTOR. Again!

Suddenly she grabs SYLVESTOR*'s hand and twirls – or he lifts her up – her confidence growing.*

KAREN. I DON'T CARE WHAT ANYONE THINKS!

MAGS *wakes up with a start.*

MAGS. What? What's happening? Who's shouting?

KAREN *stops, abruptly. Shrinks back.*

Jesus, Mary and Joseph – what's the time? Mrs Nugent gets very highly strung when there's guests.

MAGS *looks at them.*

Did you find something?

KAREN *glances at* SYLVESTOR *uncertain, but he nods at her, encouraging.*

SYLVESTOR. Oh I think we found something alright.

KAREN *hesitates.*

MAGS. Good. And they meet Mrs Nugent's requirements?

SYLVESTOR. The moment she put them on they looked – just right. Didn't they, Karen?

KAREN *hesitates.*

MAGS. Has she gone quiet again? Poor thing. Here – give me a look at them.

KAREN *glances at* SYLVESTOR, *nervous.*

She self-consciously takes a step towards MAGS.

MAGS *squints.*

Well, I can't see from here! Take them off, let me have a feel.

KAREN, *slowly, takes off one of the red shoes and tentatively comes towards* MAGS.

She's about to hand it over when SYLVESTOR *suddenly grabs the boring black shoes from earlier and swaps it for the red one in* KAREN's *hand.* KAREN *looks at him, unsure.*

But he holds his finger to his lips.

KAREN *smiles. Then she quickly hands the boring shoe to* MAGS.

MAGS *feels it.*

Seems good, sensible… What about the colour?

SYLVESTOR. The colour's the best part. Turns out it was her mother's favourite.

MAGS *looks up – does she sense some danger?*

MAGS. Oh? And what colour's that?

And KAREN *can't contain herself any longer.*

KAREN. They're the most beautiful shoes I've ever seen, Mags.

And MAGS *is suddenly worried.*

MAGS. Beautiful things can draw attention, Karen. Not always good.

SYLVESTOR. Passion has its price, the girl knows that.

He winks at KAREN.

MAGS. But some things can be beautiful in a quiet way, in a way that other people don't notice so much. Remember what I said about Mrs Nugent?

SYLVESTOR. Mrs Nugent isn't here.

MAGS. Yes but –

SYLVESTOR. The girl has the right to make her choice.

MAGS. I know that but –

SYLVESTOR (*firm*). So why not let her make it.

KAREN *takes* MAGS*'s hand, imploring.*

KAREN. Please, Mags. They'll be the nicest thing I've ever owned.

And MAGS *feels she can't argue. A beat. Then she relents.*

MAGS.... Very well. If you're sure –

SYLVESTOR. Fabulous! – I'll box them up.

He turns. Suddenly –

KAREN.... Wait!

MAGS *looks up, hopeful.*

MAGS. What? Have you changed you mind?

KAREN. I was just thinking… maybe I could wear them home.

SYLVESTOR. Well, would you look at that. She's in love with them already.

He grins.

MAGS *looks at* KAREN, *face creased with worry.*

Six

The ENSEMBLE *might appear to do the scene change –*
singing all or part of the mirror song.

ENSEMBLE. Mirror mirror, on the wall

   Keep my complexion smooth and my waistline small.

   Looking glass, what do you see

   When I'm looking at you I'm looking at me

   Show me what you have to hide

   I can see the surface

   But what's inside?

Seven

MARIELLA*'s dressing room.*

MARIELLA *is standing in front of the mirror in a fantastically*
opulent gown.

She tries to smile. It's not convincing. She lifts a bit of skin
above her eyes – clearly considering a facelift.

BOB *comes to the door, very smartly dressed.*

BOB. What time are these people getting here?

MARIELLA. Any minute now.

BOB. This collar's itching. It's driving me mad.

   She steps out, does a twirl.

MARIELLA. How do I look?

   He studies her, trying to decipher what's different about her.

BOB. Did I buy you that dress?

MARIELLA. *I* bought it.

BOB. With my credit card?

MARIELLA. Well, obviously, Bob, yes.

He shrugs indifferent.

BOB. How many times have I told you – tell me before you use that thing. It's supposed to be for expenses.

MARIELLA *deflates*.

…You look nice.

MARIELLA (*dry*). Thanks.

BOB. Did I say the wrong thing?

MARIELLA. Usually, Bob, yes.

BOB. What do you want me to say?

MARIELLA. Time was you said all manner of nice things.

BOB. Time was I had more time.

He laughs nervously. She turns away.

Should I open some wine or something?

MARIELLA *puts on some earrings or something*.

MARIELLA. Funny, isn't it? There's four of us now. We always said we wanted a bigger brood.

BOB. Did we?

MARIELLA. Once upon a time. Funny how you're trying and trying for so long and then one day you just… stop.

BOB *shifts, uncomfortable*.

BOB. Yeah. Well, we've probably saved ourselves a fortune in the long run. Clothes, toys, holidays. Look at the positives. If we'd gone and had more children… we never could've afforded the chandelier.

She stares at him sadly.

He shifts, uncomfortable.

I'll open the wine.

He turns to go.

MARIELLA. Bob?

BOB. Yeah?

MARIELLA.…Why don't we dance any more?

They lock eyes for a beat, something unspoken between them.

Then he shrugs it off.

BOB. You and your rhetorical questions… See you downstairs.

He goes.

MARIELLA *is alone.*

She looks at her reflection on the mirror, tries to gather herself.

MARIELLA. Mirror mirror, on the wall… how do I look today?

MIRROR (*perfunctory*). You look great today – Mariella.

MARIELLA. Oh shut up.

Music.

She turns towards us and sings.

Mariella's aria: 'How Am I Here?'

On my wedding day I married my prince
But the truth is I haven't seen that man since
Where is the boy whose heart I made sing
Where is the man who gave me this ring?

On my wedding day I married my Bob
I loved him so much, that I gave up my job
He said he'd be true, that he'd always be kind
I never imagined I'd be left behind.

Between life and its problems, the jigs and the reels
Between daily existence and property deals.
He's been distracted and he's disappeared
My life's contracted yet I'm somehow here
How am I here?

Beat.

At least I've got the chandelieeeer.

CLIVE *appears behind her holding the axe.*

She goes to sing again.

CLIVE. Mom?

MARIELLA *jumps.*

MARIELLA. For God's sake, Clive – don't creep up on me like that – what if I was naked?

CLIVE. Where's the orphan?

MARIELLA. How should I know? I've more important things on my mind.

A doorbell rings.

MARIELLA *jumps, panicked.*

It's them! They're here… How do I look?

CLIVE *shrugs.*

CLIVE. Same as always.

MARIELLA. Right.

CLIVE. I'll check the other room.

He goes.

MARIELLA *looks at herself in the mirror one last time. Sings the last line.*

MARIELLA (*sung*).
    How am I here?

She goes.

Eight

A long dining table with a white dining cloth.

MARIELLA, BOB, *the* PRIEST, CLIVE *and the* ENSEMBLE
of dinner GUESTS *are there – perhaps poised with glasses.*
(*Once again they speak somewhat chorally as needed.*)

BOB *is holding court – ready to perform a trick.*

BOB. You wouldn't necessarily make the connection but
    property development and magic actually have a lot in
    common. Not that I call myself a property developer, but for
    the sake of argument – it's the same guiding principle.
    Distraction.

*He holds up a twenty-euro note and a pencil. He folds the
note up into a small square through the following.*

For example, I go to the relevant people – the county
    council, the banks, et cetera – and I say look over here, look
    over here – there's a great opportunity. So they look over
    there. And then I say –

He closes his hand around the note.

*He takes out a pencil and pretends to use it as a wand over
the hand with the twenty euro in it.*

On the count of three – something magic is going to happen.
    Well, I don't say that to *them* obviously, I'm being
    metaphorical but you get the idea – (*Counting, tapping his
    closed hand with the pencil each time.*) One, two / –

GUESTS/BOB. Two… Three!

On the 'three' the pencil disappears.

BOB. See?

GUESTS. Ooh.

BOB. And before they know it, there's a luxury apartment block
    standing where some run-down community library no one
    cared about once was.

He pulls the pencil down from behind his ear.

And a car park thrown in for good measure.

GUESTS. Aaah.

But he opens his hand – the twenty euro has disappeared.

BOB. And no one even saw it going up.

They clap.

MARIELLA (*tense*). Very good, very good. Now –

BOB. Will I show them the one with the napkin? That always
gets a laugh. Wait'll you see this. Napkin, spoon.

*He does something vaguely obscene with a spoon and
a napkin.*

MARIELLA *laughs, slightly hysterical.*

MARIELLA. Isn't that – fabulous. (*Whispering*.) Enough now,
Bob. (*To* GUESTS.) Of course we didn't invite you here
tonight for magic tricks. No, we invited you here to this –
culinary feast for a much more important reason…

She makes a 'gravely important' gesture.

…to meet the orphan we rescued from devastating
impoverishment.

CLIVE. You mean Karen?

MARIELLA. Yes, I mean Karen.

PRIEST. I must say, Mrs Nugent, we in the town are so
heartened by the Christian charity you and your family have
shown to the girl.

GUEST 1. Yes /

GUEST 2. Wonderful /

GUEST 3. Very kind.

PRIEST. She didn't have the greatest start in life.

The GUESTS *shake their heads in empathy, as* MARIELLA
nods graciously.

MARIELLA. Well, it's all too easy to sit by and do nothing
these days, Father. You walk past a homeless person or
a drunk in the street and naturally you think – they got
themselves into that mess, if they don't have the wherewithal

to put the bottle down and get a decent job – isn't it their own fault they are where they are? But when you dig a little deeper and look a little closer – you remember that we're all of us vulnerable to the vagaries of fate. I mean, if Bob's business closed tomorrow… well, we'd probably be fine – we have some investments, but that's not the point. The point is you never know. You just never know.

MAGS, *who has been filling the glasses, looks up*.

MAGS (*dry*). An excellent point, Mrs Nugent. You've a philosophical mind.

MARIELLA (*surprised*). Thank you, Mags.

GUEST 1. Yes /

GUEST 2. Wonderful /

GUEST 4. Very philosophical.

MAGS *shuffles off to the kitchen*.

MARIELLA. Of course we'd heard the whispers about Karen's mother long before she passed.

CLIVE *perks up, intrigued*.

CLIVE. What whispers?

BOB. That she was off her trolley.

MARIELLA. Bob!

BOB. Am I wrong?

PRIEST. She was a troubled woman, Mr Nugent, there's no doubt about that. Of course she wasn't from here. No family or support. And some of the things they say she got up to to make ends meet –

MARIELLA *nods sagely*.

CLIVE (*intrigued*). What things did she get up to?

They all glance at one another. An unmentionable.

PRIEST. Let's just say she strayed from the flock.

CLIVE. Which flock?

MARIELLA. Don't probe, Clive. My son has a very morbid imagination. Luckily he channels it into his art.

PRIEST. All the greats do.

BOB. Well, that's what we hope, otherwise we've got a bit of a psycho on our hands, what?

He laughs.

MARIELLA *glares at him.* BOB *pats* CLIVE *on the back.*

I've tried to interest him in the rugby but –

CLIVE. It's a masculine cliché.

GUEST 1. Well, I must say I marvel at your courage, Mariella. A teenage orphan –

GUEST 2. With a volatile family history.

GUEST 3. Yes /

GUEST 4. Brave /

GUEST 2. Very.

The GUESTS *all nod, sagely.* MARIELLA *is thrilled.*

GUEST 1. You know I think we could get some publicity around this!

MARIELLA. Oh no. We're not at all interested in publicity are we, Bob?… Unless of course it helps the Foundation. Anything to help the Foundation – I'm still waiting to hear about my application. Any word on that?

The GUESTS *ignore her.*

GUEST 2. We could send out a press release.

GUEST 3. Yes! /

GUEST 1. A picture of you and Bob and Karen!

MARIELLA. Well, I wouldn't think she's all that photogenic –

BOB. Where is she anyway?

MARIELLA. Who?

BOB. The orphan.

   MARIELLA looks around.

MARIELLA. I thought she was here.

BOB (*calling*). Mags! Where's the orphan?

   MAGS comes out of the kitchen wiping her hands on her apron.

MAGS....I haven't seen her since we came back from the shoemaker's. She was so pleased with her new shoes, Mrs Nugent, all the way home she was skipping and laughing and praising your kindness at letting her pick whatever pair she liked.

   MARIELLA glances at MAGS, sharp.

MARIELLA. What?

   But the GUESTS are thrilled.

GUEST 1. Beautiful /

GUEST 2. Wonderful /

GUEST 4. To bring a child such joy.

MARIELLA. Well, you should have seen what she was wearing when she came to us. Practically rags, wasn't it, Father?

PRIEST. Her mother used to make all her clothes. She was quite a talented seamstress at one time.

CLIVE. Before she lost her mind?

MARIELLA. Well, there wasn't much talent in what I saw, I can tell you. Some of it bordered on the obscene. But Mags and I took her in hand and found her something much more –

   Suddenly KAREN comes to the door. She's wearing the red shoes. She smiles at the GUESTS.

KAREN. Hello.

   MARIELLA's eyes stray to her shoes.

MARIELLA....Suitable.

Everyone turns to look at KAREN. *There's something different – a confidence about her. Maybe she's made her baggy dress shorter or sexier, or maybe she's wearing her hair a different way. But either way it should be very apparent.*

BOB (*surprised*). Karen! Wow… You look – different.

MARIELLA *glances at him, sharp.*

MARIELLA. Doesn't she?

KAREN. Mrs Nugent bought me a new pair of shoes.

She comes into the room, does a little twirl.

Aren't they pretty?

The GUESTS *lean down for a closer look.*

GUEST 1. Hmmn /

GUEST 2. Yes. /

GUEST 3. Most unusual.

PRIEST. And you picked them out yourself?

MARIELLA *opens her mouth to speak.*

But KAREN *gets there first.*

KAREN. It was all Mrs Nugent's idea. She sent me to a shoemaker – one of the best in the world.

GUEST 1. Really? /

GUEST 2. Wonderful /

GUEST 4. Very kind.

The GUESTS *look at* MARIELLA *who smiles tightly.*

MARIELLA. Only the best for our Karen. Sit down, Karen. Quickly. Everyone's been dying to meet you.

KAREN. In a minute.

MARIELLA *is shocked.*

MARIELLA. Sorry?

KAREN. What I mean is… there's something I'd like to do first.

MARIELLA. What sort of something?

MARIELLA *laughs*.

She didn't talk so much when she first came to us. Takes some getting used to.

KAREN. I was thinking I might perform.

MARIELLA. Perform!

GUEST 1. Oh /

GUEST 2. Interesting /

GUEST 3. Very good.

MARIELLA. But what on earth would you perform?

KAREN *smiles sweetly*.

KAREN. I was thinking… I could dance. For your guests.

MARIELLA (*horrified*). Dance! No honestly, Karen, there's no need for that.

KAREN *looks at the* GUESTS.

KAREN. My mother was a dancer.

GUEST 1. Really? /

GUEST 2. Was she? /

GUEST 4. Most unusual /

MARIELLA. 'Dancer' more like.

KAREN. She taught me a bit. The other night when you asked me to show you, I felt a bit shy –

MARIELLA. Understandable.

KAREN. But now I feel better –

MARIELLA. Well, best not to push it.

KAREN (*determined*). Now I feel confident.

MARIELLA. There's really no / need.

GUEST 1. If she wants to dance, why not let her?

BOB. No listen we've seen it before.

He makes a 'it's dire' hand gesture. But KAREN*'s determined.*

KAREN. But now I think I could be good. Please, Mr and Mrs Nugent. I'd like to try.

And MARIELLA *is backed into a corner. She relents.*

MARIELLA.... Very well. If you must.

She sits down, awkwardly.

KAREN *smiles.*

She comes into the centre of the room and stands before the GUESTS, *who watch her with keen interest.*

Suddenly, music. The strains of something faintly tango-ish from somewhere, off.

Do the lights change too?

KAREN *starts to move with the music towards the table. Slow at first but gaining confidence.*

As the music starts to become more sultry, KAREN*'s movements become sensual, seductive. Nothing like before.*

MARIELLA *watches open-mouthed – as* KAREN *begins to circle the table.*

As she continues we start to realise that BOB *is watching* KAREN *closely, slightly mesmerised by her or the shoes.* KAREN *stops beside him.*

....What are you...?

KAREN *beckons* BOB *with her finger.*

BOB (*surprised*). Me?

And almost like he's hypnotised, BOB *suddenly stands up.*

MARIELLA *tries to stop him –*

MARIELLA (*hissing*). Bob. Stop it. Sit down!

But he doesn't.

KAREN *puts her hand out and he takes it.*

A few tentative steps as he finds his feet… then suddenly BOB *and* KAREN *are going full tango around the dining table.*

BOB *is brilliant, assured, better then we could have imagined.*

As the GUESTS *watch, stunned,* BOB *and* KAREN*'s dance becomes faster, and more dangerous – the two of them moving sensually in time with the music.*

BOB *dips* KAREN*, or she dips him, he lifts her up, they move apart, then back together again.*

MARIELLA *tries to bring it to an end.*

Alright…

But they continue.

KAREN*'s thrilled.*

BOB*'s exhilarated.* MARIELLA *claps again trying to stop it.*

That's really quite…

But they continue. It seems like they might never stop.

Suddenly MARIELLA *stands up, furious.*

THAT'S ENOUGH OF THAT!

The music cuts out.

BOB *and* KAREN *spring apart.*

(*Clipped.*) Thank you, Karen, I think we get the gist.

BOB *suddenly seems quite mortified.* KAREN *looks a little unsure.*

CLIVE *bursts into applause. Maybe one or two* GUESTS *join in, uncertain.*

CLIVE. That was killer, Dad!

BOB *loosens his tie.*

BOB. Was it yeah?

PRIEST. I had no idea you could dance like that, Mr Nugent.

BOB. Well, I haven't in years really. What with my lower back.

MARIELLA. Your lower back, is it?

He glances at KAREN, *loosens his tie.*

BOB. S'pose it's just a bit of fun.

MARIELLA. Well, we're not here for a bit of fun, are we?
We're here to think about orphans. Sit down please, Bob.

BOB *walks sheepishly to his place.*

MARIELLA *smiles, tightly at the* GUESTS.

As you can see she's had a traumatic upbringing. Hopefully
a loving home will set her right. (*To* KAREN.) Come to the
table please, dear.

KAREN *starts to walk to the table but her feet grind to
a stop.*

She looks down confused.

She tries to walk forward again.

They stop again.

MAGS *enters with a large pot of soup or a jug of water or
something.*

MAGS. Here we are – just what the doctor ordered.

She puts things down on the table.

Karen, come on and take a seat, love.

KAREN *tries again to walk to the table.*

But it's like she's glued to the floor.

KAREN. I can't…

MAGS. What?

MARIELLA. What are you talking about?

KAREN *looks at them worried.*

KAREN....My feet... they won't move.

MARIELLA. What do you mean, they won't move?

Suddenly KAREN*'s feet spring to life and rush her away from the table.*

KAREN. Whoa...

MARIELLA. Stop this messing, Karen, and sit down. Honestly I don't know what's gotten into her.

KAREN*'s feet do it again. She teeters around the room.*

KAREN. I swear it's not me.

MARIELLA. I'm going to lose my temper in a minute.

MAGS *looks at* KAREN, *worried.*

MAGS. Karen, please, you're upsetting Mrs Nugent.

But KAREN *keeps moving.*

KAREN. I can't help it.

MARIELLA *puts down her napkin.*

MARIELLA (*exasperated*). Right. I'll have to come and get you, is that it?

MARIELLA *comes out from behind the table and forcefully grabs* KAREN *by the arm.*

Silly girl. Come here.

Suddenly KAREN*'s foot rises up and kicks* MARIELLA *in the shin.*

Ow!

MARIELLA *stumbles backward, stunned.*

She just... kicked me!

PRIEST (*shocked*). Karen!

KAREN....I didn't mean to, I swear.

MARIELLA *goes to grab her again.*

MARIELLA (*angry*). Now look here, young lady!

  KAREN *kicks her again.*

(*Disbelief.*) She did it again!

KAREN. It isn't me!

PRIEST. Karen, come on. Pull yourself together – ow!

  KAREN *kicks him too.*

MAGS. What's happening?

CLIVE (*gleeful*). The orphan's going nuts!

  KAREN *jumps up onto a chair.*

MARIELLA. Get down from there!

KAREN. It's the shoes.

  MAGS *worried, moves towards* KAREN.

MAGS. Please, love, remember what we said.

BOB. Is she having some kind of fit?

  And suddenly KAREN *jumps up onto the middle of the*
  dining table. She starts to hopscotch up and down the table.

MARIELLA. No! That's the good china, Karen!

MAGS. Please, Karen, stop. You'll get yourself in trouble.

  Suddenly, KAREN *begins to kick things off the table.*
  Glasses, plates, cutlery…

  Music.

  And almost in some sort of slow motion we watch as the
  following carnage takes place:

  KAREN *kicks a knife.*

  It travels through the air slowly and hits the PRIEST *in*
  the arm.

  He falls to the ground.

  KAREN *kicks a fork, it vaults through the air and hits*
  CLIVE *in the eye.*

He screams and stumbles backwards.

Another knife hits MARIELLA.

MARIELLA. Ahhh!

KAREN *kicks a spoon.*

It flies through the air and hits BOB *in the face.*

Everyone at the table – including the GUESTS – *have been hit or are reeling from the assault. Some of them are staggering, some are falling, some are picking themselves up.*

KAREN *looks around her, shocked at what she's done.*

Then the shoes make KAREN *do one last large jump in the middle of the table.*

As KAREN*'s feet hit the table with a BANG the cutlery everyone is holding drops to the floor with a CLANG.*

Silence.

Everyone looks at KAREN *in shock.*

Suddenly at the back of the room, MAGS *lets out a cry.*

MAGS. Oh my chest…

MAGS *staggers forward a few steps.*

I've a terrible pain… I can't… oh.

Suddenly MAGS *collapses onto the ground.*

MARIELLA. Mags!… Bob, quick. I think she's having a heart attack.

BOB. What? Are you sure? Mags! Can you hear me? Mags!

MARIELLA. Is she breathing?

BOB *kneels down and listens for* MAGS*'s breath.*

BOB. I can't hear anything –

KAREN *pulls the shoes off and jumps down from the table, concerned for* MAGS.

KAREN. Is she alright?

MARIELLA *turns on her.*

MARIELLA. Look what you've done. This is all your fault.

KAREN stares at MAGS, terrified.

KAREN. It wasn't me, it was the shoes.

MARIELLA comes at her, furious.

MARIELLA. The shoes! The shoes!

MARIELLA slaps KAREN hard across the face.

The GUESTS all gasp.

That's what you get for barefaced lies!

KAREN staggers backwards, shocked.

MARIELLA turns away, upset.

Where's the phone? I'll call the doctor.

As MARIELLA rushes off, in the background BOB performs CPR on MAGS.

BOB. Come on, Mags. Hang in there…

KAREN stands clutching her face, she looks at the red shoes on the ground.

The PRIEST comes towards her. Something knowing in his face. Is he smiling at her? The way SYLVESTOR smiled?

The PRIEST leans down and picks up the shoes.

Just as CLIVE picks up a guitar in the corner and walks towards us, strumming gently –

The PRIEST places the shoes neatly on the table. They twinkle in the light.

Then he looks at KAREN and winks.

CLIVE steps out to the front of the stage and starts to sing:

Clive's song: 'We're All Dead Inside'.

> We're all dead inside
> When did you last cry?
> I cut things up so I can find
> Why we're all dead inside.

The red curtain drops behind him.

> We're all dead inside
> I can't empathise
> I don't relate so I mutilate
> Cos I feel dead inside.
>
> Some people jump from planes
> Others love ghost trains
> Maybe for you it's the roll of the dice
> But for me it's torturing mice
> I hear them squeal, I know it's real
> It's the only way I feel.

Do the taxidermy animals appear behind him singing through the curtain?

> We're all dead inside
> There's no place to hide
> Suspended in formaldehyde
> We're all dead inside.

SYLVESTOR *appears and takes the guitar off him.*

CLIVE *walks off.*

SYLVESTOR. Thank you very much, ladies and gentlemen. That'll be the interval.

ACT TWO

Nine

SYLVESTOR *walks onto the stage again. Is he wearing the red shoes now?*

He smiles at us. Something knowing.

Then –

SYLVESTOR. Hey diddle diddle

We've got to the middle

And what is our orphan to do?

She's got the shoes that she dreamed of

But all's not what it seems, love

She might yet lose a foot

Or two.

He laughs loudly, sinister.

It fills the auditorium.

He stops.

Silence.

Then he breaks into a little tap dance.

The curtain raises a little and we might see a couple of red stilettos dancing with him – the music cheerful, happy.

The music cuts out.

SYLVESTOR *looks at us.*

Right, let's get on with it, shall we?

He pulls up the curtain.

*KAREN, BOB and MARIELLA are behind it. The shoes –
behind them on the table.*

It's later that night, BOB *and* MARIELLA *are just back
from hospital.*

SYLVESTOR *puts on his* PRIEST*'s collar and steps into
the action.*

PRIEST. Mrs Nugent, what a terrible ordeal!

MARIELLA. I've never been so upset in my life.

PRIEST. Mags is like family to you.

MARIELLA. Mags? Oh – yes. But Mags'll be fine /

BOB. Well, she's in intensive care.

MARIELLA. Yes /

BOB. Hooked up to a heart monitor.

MARIELLA. But she'll be fine. And if she's not, they'll
resuscitate her. What can't be resuscitated is my reputation.
I'll never forgot the look on that chairwoman's face when
she saw me slap Karen. As if *I'm* the monster.

She points to KAREN, *furious.*

She's the monster! She drove me to it /

BOB. Now let's just calm down.

MARIELLA. You can't hit an orphan in front of the Save the
Orphans Foundation, Bob – you're supposed to be saving
them. My application's ruined. They'll never have me now.
Wicked girl!

MARIELLA *comes at* KAREN *again, the* PRIEST *steps
between them.*

PRIEST. In the child's defence, Mrs Nugent, it doesn't seem
like she was in her right mind.

MARIELLA. Which you assured us wouldn't be an issue, Father.

PRIEST. Well, yes –

MARIELLA. You said she was stable!

PRIEST And she is – for the most part.

BOB. So what – do we need a psychiatrist or an exorcist now?

BOB *laughs weakly.*

The PRIEST *tries to appeal.*

PRIEST. I agree that, like her mother, the girl seems to have a – wayward streak. But unlike her mother, there is still hope for her. With you and Mr Nugent's guidance –

MARIELLA. If guidance is what she needs, she might be better off with you, Father –

PRIEST (*alarmed*). Oh God, no. I don't want her.

He glances at KAREN *and gathers himself.*

What I mean is, she must learn by example. And what better example than to be nestled in the bosom of a family.

MARIELLA. Well, I'm not clutching a viper to my bosom twice.

PRIEST. Mrs Nugent, she's hardly a viper. Look at her.

KAREN *tries to look sweet.*

MARIELLA. I'm sick of looking at her! And that sorrow round the eyes seems a lot more sinister now. To think she had the nerve to blame the shoes *I* bought her out of the goodness of *my* heart –

PRIEST. Mrs Nugent –

MARIELLA *rubs her eyes.*

MARIELLA. Oh I can't talk about it any more – I need a bath and a face mask. We can decide what to do with her in the morning.

BOB. S'pose we'll have to put you in the spare, Father.

PRIEST. If it's not too much trouble…

MARIELLA. Well, even if it was, we'd still have to. Follow me, Father. (*To* BOB, *sharp*.) Bob, don't linger!

BOB. I'm coming…

MARIELLA *snatches the red shoes up off the table –*

MARIELLA. I'll take these!

– and gives KAREN *one last withering glance.*

No excuses now, is there, madam!

She stalks off, followed by the PRIEST.

BOB *glances at* KAREN, *awkward. Starts to go.*

KAREN....Mr Nugent?

BOB *turns back – making sure* MARIELLA*'s not near.*

BOB. How did you do it?

KAREN *looks at him blankly.*

KAREN....What?

BOB. The dancing. How did you do it? I haven't moved like that in years. The energy, the electricity –

KAREN. You felt it too?

BOB. Surged right through me. Was like a young man again. I could have leapt on that table, danced all night.

KAREN *looks at him, amazed.*

KAREN. I know!

BOB. Did you slip something in my drink?

KAREN. No... it was the shoes.

BOB (*disbelief*). Come on, it's just me here, you can tell the truth.

KAREN. I *am* telling the truth... it was the shoes.

BOB *studies her, confused.*

A dangerous thought suddenly occurs.

BOB. Oh no. Oh no no no I've heard about this. Men my age. First they buy the convertible – (*Gasps.*) then it's the hair plugs –

He puts a hand up to his hair, worried.

Then the leather jacket, then they're up all night, in the clubs with younger –

He looks at her horrified.

And a *tan*! Oh no. No no, no, no. Not Bob Nugent. I will not be drawn in to some midlife –

He steps away from her quickly. She follows him.

KAREN. I didn't mean to cause trouble.

BOB. Well.

He steps away again.

KAREN. What happened at the table – wasn't me.

BOB. Certainly looked like you.

KAREN. But it wasn't. At least… it didn't feel like me.

She looks up at him, suddenly worried.

Although… my mother used to say that when she danced she didn't feel like herself either.

BOB. Your mother?

KAREN. She said it just came through her like a force… Do you think the shoes made me like that? Like her?

BOB. I don't –

She comes towards him, anxious.

KAREN. People keep saying she wasn't right in the head…
I always thought she was perfect but maybe…

She looks at him sadly.

…maybe I just couldn't see.

BOB. I'm really not the person to talk to about this.

KAREN. Are you going to send me away?

BOB. You need to take that up with /

KAREN (*desperate*). Please don't! Please – I want to stay…
Mariella's the nicest woman I've ever met.

BOB*'s astonished.*

BOB. Well, that's… Really? How many people have you met?

KAREN. Will you tell her I'm sorry?

BOB. Look –

KAREN. Will you tell her I'll do anything to make it right?

BOB. I can't /

KAREN (*desperate*). I'll clean the house. I'll cook, I'll do whatever she wants. I won't put a foot wrong again I swear. Just ask her – please – beg, beg her to give me a second chance.

And BOB *can't help but be affected.*

Please, Mr Nugent… You're all that I have.

He considers for a moment. Is his interest entirely innocent?

BOB. Well, I suppose I could… have a word.

KAREN. Oh thank you.

She rushes to give him a hug, but he backs away quickly.

BOB. No that's – fine. That's alright. You – stay over there.

Beat.

Not making any promises now.

KAREN. I know.

BOB. I'll only talk to her.

KAREN. Okay.

BOB. Okay. Well…

He turns to go.

KAREN.…Mr Nugent?

He turns back.

BOB (*wary*). Yes, Karen?

KAREN. Did you… like the shoes on me?

BOB. Did I like them?

KAREN. You looked at me differently when I wore them, that's all. It made me think that… maybe you did?

BOB takes a breath. Trying to decide how to answer.

BOB. Oh. Well, yes, I suppose I – liked them. But you must never say that to Mrs Nugent.

KAREN. Why not?

BOB. You just mustn't. Ever. Ever ever ever ever. Okay?

KAREN (*confused*). Okay.

He glances at her one more time. A touch of longing.

BOB. Maybe when you're older you'll… understand.

Beat.

Goodnight, Karen.

KAREN. Goodnight, Mr Nugent.

He goes.

KAREN is alone.

She looks down at her feet. She feels strange.

A beat.

Maybe she makes a movement, tries to dance… but without the shoes, she can't.

She stops and looks down at her feet, deflated.

Ten

The Red Shoes Interlude

Night.

Very late.

Music.

MARIELLA*'s dressing room.*

The red shoes sit on a table – twinkling.

MARIELLA *in a face mask, hair-rollers and a dressing gown, creeps into the room.*

She looks around to make sure no one's watching her.

Then she goes to the shoes and examines them carefully.

She holds them up to the light – as if trying to determine if there is anything magic about them.

MARIELLA (*mimicking* KAREN). 'The shoes made me do it!' Little liar…

> *She puts the shoes back and is about to head out when an idea occurs.*
>
> *She puts the shoes on the ground and tries to squeeze her foot into one of them.*
>
> *Then the other.*
>
> *Suddenly from outside –*

BOB. Mariella!

MARIELLA *jumps.*

MARIELLA. Coming!

> *She puts the shoes back where they were and rushes out.*
>
> *A second later,* BOB *comes in.*
>
> *He sees the shoes on the ground.*
>
> *He looks around.*
>
> *For a second he contemplates putting them on. But he shakes off the idea…*

He picks them up.

He looks at himself in the mirror, admiring himself.

Then he holds one in each hand as if they were the hands of a dancing partner, and closes his eyes. He begins to dance a kind of salsa with the shoes.

Suddenly –

(*Off.*) Bob! What are you doing?

BOB *puts the shoes back and rushes out.*

BOB (*as he goes*). Nothing! I was just… tidying up.

A second later KAREN *creeps in in her nightdress.*

She looks at the shoes, nervous.

She turns to check no one is behind her.

Then she picks them up – admiring them.

She puts them on the ground, then lifts her foot above one shoe.

It hovers there as she weighs up whether to put them on.

Suddenly CLIVE *appears in the doorway with an axe.*

CLIVE. You're not allowed in here!

KAREN *jumps.*

And you're definitely not allowed to wear those.

KAREN. I know. I was just going to bed.

KAREN *puts the shoes back and looks at* CLIVE.

CLIVE *lifts his axe, threatening and* KAREN *rushes out.*

CLIVE *walks towards the shoes.*

He inspects them, unimpressed, then lifts his axe to chop one in half.

He brings it down with force – but misses. Does the shoe move?

CLIVE *looks at them in disgust*.

CLIVE. Stupid shoes…

He takes his axe and stalks out.

Eleven

MAGS *is wheeled in on a bed/hospital gurney.*

CLIVE (*off*). How's your ticker, Mags?

MAGS. Well, it's still ticking anyway. For the time being.

CLIVE *enters.*

CLIVE. Did they give you an electric shock?

MAGS (*horrified*). What?

CLIVE. They usually do when your heart stops, they have these machines with an electric current, they put them on your chest and BOOM – you're alive again.

He mimes it. MAGS *shrinks back.*

MAGS. I'd punch any doctor who did that to me.

CLIVE. Do it to the brains of crazy people too. Electric-shock them into being normal.

MARIELLA *enters.*

Karen's mother probably had that. Maybe Karen could have some too after what she did to all the good china.

MARIELLA. Alright that's enough. Go and make Mags a cup of tea.

CLIVE. Thought that's the orphan's job.

MARIELLA. Go!

He heads out, annoyed. MARIELLA *smiles and fusses with* MAGS*'s bedclothes.*

We're so pleased to have you home again, Mags.

MAGS. Well, I'm pleased to be home /

MARIELLA. And really it's no burden at all to have to look after you day in and day out, while getting nothing in return, you mustn't give it a second thought.

MAGS (*hesitant*).… alright.

MARIELLA. Obviously when the doctor said you were going to require round-the-clock care, we *were* a bit – alarmed. For you. After all, who was there to do it? Bob's up to his eyes in this casino business and my life's jam-packed with – meetings and the like. But then the most wonderful solution presented itself…

MAGS.…Oh?

KAREN *enters dutifully wearing a white carer's uniform. She smiles at* MAGS.

MAGS *looks at* MARIELLA *shocked.*

…Karen?

MARIELLA. Now, don't you worry, she's not going to try any more of her funny business. If she so much as puts one toe out of place – she's straight off to the foster home – isn't that right, Karen?

KAREN *nods, grimly.*

I had made up my mind to send her back earlier, but Bob said the Foundation might like it if we turned the other cheek. And I've got good cheekbones so…

MAGS. But is it fair to the girl?

MARIELLA. Fair! She's lucky she's not out on her ear.

MAGS. But she shouldn't be cooped up here with me. She's just a child.

MARIELLA. Nonsense! She didn't seem like a child when she was dancing round the dinner table with my husband, did she? She'll make you meals, she'll clean your bedpan, she'll sleep right here on the floor, so if there's ever anything you want or need, Karen can be sure to get it.

MAGS *looks at* KAREN, *worried*.

MAGS. But –

MARIELLA (*excited*). You haven't heard the best part yet, Mags. Bob was right. The chairwoman of Save the Orphans rang just this morning – and asked me to lunch! Imagine! If we'd given Karen away I'd have had nothing to talk to her about, but now… You reap what you sow, Mags, you reap what you sow.

MARIELLA *does a little jump for joy*.

Then looks at KAREN, *sharp*.

You. Clean that up.

KAREN *scurries to clean up some invisible spillage*.

MAGS. What happened to the shoes?

MARIELLA *gives* KAREN *a withering look*.

MARIELLA. The shoes? People who lie and cheat and behave like animals don't get nice shoes. People who behave like that don't get anything nice, do they, Karen?

KAREN *looks down, ashamed*.

KAREN. No, Mrs Nugent.

MARIELLA. I'll be back later. (*To* KAREN.) Clean up this room, it's like a pigsty.

MARIELLA *goes*.

MAGS *looks at* KAREN, *concerned*.

MAGS. This is all my fault.

KAREN *starts fluffing* MAGS's *pillows*.

KAREN. Don't be silly, Mags.

MAGS. …I never should've let you buy those damn shoes.

KAREN. I wanted them. Sure you couldn't even see them.

MAGS *looks at her, sheepish*.

MAGS. Well… that's not – quite true. I just wanted you to have something nice.

KAREN. I don't understand…

MAGS. You don't always need eyes to see things, Karen.

KAREN*'s confused.* MAGS *mulls how to explain. Then –*

…Mr Nugent! Could you come in here for a sec?

BOB *enters with his phone.*

BOB. I'm waiting on a call, Mags. We've an international investor, loves the casino idea –

MAGS. You wouldn't have a deck of cards on you, by any chance?

BOB. Cards?

He reaches into his pocket, pulls out a deck.

Always come prepared, Mags – magician's code. Want to see a trick?

MAGS. Actually… I've a trick to show you, Mr Nugent. If you don't mind.

BOB (*surprised*). Didn't know you were in to magic, Mags.

MAGS. There's a lot about me you mightn't know, Mr Nugent. Now. Shuffle the deck and pick out a card – but don't let me see it.

BOB. Right-ho –

He shuffles expertly and picks a card.

MAGS. Ready?

BOB. Yup.

BOB *shows* KAREN *the card, then holds it up for the audience.*

MAGS *concentrates, trying to visualise.*

MAGS. It's red… triangular… diamonds! Ace of diamonds.

BOB *looks at the card impressed.*

BOB. Not bad… Can you do it again though?

BOB *shuffles the cards again. Shows* KAREN *another card.*

MAGS *concentrates*.

MAGS. This one's black… round… a six… or nine of clubs!

BOB *looks at the card*.

BOB. Six of clubs… Alright. Let me see if I can figure how you –

He shuffles again and is about to pull one more –

MAGS. Jack of spades!

BOB. Hold your horses. I haven't even…

He pulls out a card. Stares at it amazed.

How d' you know?

MAGS. That one just came to me clear as day. Sometimes it works like that.

BOB. Do you have them marked or something?

MAGS.…It's a gift. Always had it.

BOB *takes this in. Beat. Then he laughs*.

BOB. A gift! You're good, Mags. They should have you in the magic circle –

A phone goes in his pocket.

Quick – use that gift to get me more money. D' you know how much it costs to cut down trees! (*Answering*.) Donny, how are ya? Seen the plans?

He heads off.

KAREN.…I didn't know you had a gift, Mags.

MAGS *leans in to* KAREN, *ominous*.

MAGS. No well… People like you and me, Karen – we have to keep our gifts to ourselves. We have to keep our heads down and our mouths shut. Otherwise… otherwise terrible things can happen. Things we can't control.

KAREN *doesn't understand what* MAGS *means*.

But before she can press her, CLIVE *comes in carrying a tray.*

CLIVE. Here's your tea.

He dumps it on the bed.

Next time, she can get it. I'm going to the forest to work on my art.

He starts to walk out.

MAGS. Take Karen with you.

CLIVE. She's s'posed to stay here and do what you say.

MAGS. Well, I say she could use some fresh air, like a normal girl her age. Go on, take her.

CLIVE *sighs loudly* –

CLIVE. Fine! (*To* KAREN.) But don't walk beside me.

CLIVE *goes.*

KAREN *hesitates, but* MAGS *gestures for her to go on and she does.*

MAGS *is left in bed alone.*

Music.

MAGS *turns to us and begins to sing.*

Mags's song: 'Invisible'.

MAGS.
	There are things I regret
	There are things I daren't mention
	I did what I had to
	Being left with no state pension
	Scrubbed a million floors
	Washed dishes till I'm raw
	I made my choice, stifled my voice
	Became invisible.

	There are things no one knows
	There are secrets I can never say
	I did what I had to
	But I did things their way
	Washed a million sinks

>Poured a million drinks
>No one asks me what I think
>Cos I'm invisible
>I'm invisible.

Does she stagger out of bed, unsteady, but roused?

>Course there are times I want to scream
>If they hand me one more pot to clean
>Shout I'm a woman, a human being
>And I had hopes and dreams
>Don't you see?

>But there are things I can't roar
>There are things that I can't talk about
>So I keep my head down
>Put the rubbish bins out
>I made my pact, now I must act
>Like I'm invisible.

She sits on the bed so exhausted and emotionally drained.

CLIVE *enters and goes to the bedside to pick up a large knife –*

CLIVE. Sorry. Forgot this.

– and he walks out again, without looking at her.

See ya.

MAGS *lies on the bed, invisible. End music.*

Twelve

CLIVE *and* KAREN *are in the forest.*

KAREN, *aware of the ghosts, looks around, uneasy.*

CLIVE *has a hunting knife.*

CLIVE. You can make a knife out of anything, you know. Bits of metal – tin of beans. You just have to know how to sharpen it.

He looks at her.

Give me your hand.

KAREN *draws back. Shakes her head.*

It's just a test. To see if the blade is blunt. Probably won't even mark you.

KAREN *hesitates. The knife looks sharp.*

KAREN. I don't want to.

CLIVE. If you let me, I won't tell Mariella you left Mags on her own.

KAREN. Mags told me to.

CLIVE. You think she'll believe that? After everything you've done?

Beat.

KAREN *reluctantly puts out her arm.*

CLIVE *holds it with one arm, lifts the knife with the other.*

SYLVESTOR *appears holding a leash and wearing a pair of glittery pink stilettos.*

SYLVESTOR. Well, hello there, children. What a pretty day!

KAREN *jumps.*

KAREN. You!

CLIVE. Do you know him?

SYLVESTOR (*to* CLIVE). Forgive me, I don't believe we've met. I'm Sylvestor. I make shoes.

CLIVE. So what are you wearing those for? (*Snigger.*) They're for girls.

SYLVESTOR. Oh dear boy.

Where's your flair?

There's more to life than Nikee Air.

CLIVE. It's pronounced Nike.

SYLVESTOR (*to* KAREN). Is he always so dull?

KAREN. I thought your shop was… that way.

She points, looks around confused.

Or… that way.

SYLVESTOR. My shop is every way, my dear. But on my lunch break, I walk the cat.

CLIVE. Who walks a cat!

SYLVESTOR. No one it seems and now I know why.

She wriggled and wriggled till she got herself loose.

Ran into the trees, the brazen strap.

(*To the cat.*) Well, you're on your own now, Manolo, I can tell you that!

CLIVE. I can find her. If you want.

SYLVESTOR. Really?

CLIVE. I'm pretty good with cats.

SYLVESTOR. How much do you charge?

CLIVE *smiles, sinister.*

CLIVE. Finders, keepers.

SYLVESTOR. Losers weepers… I think I understand you.

SYLVESTOR *studies* CLIVE.

Alright. If you find her, you can keep her.

CLIVE. Yes!

CLIVE *rushes off, delighted.*

SYLVESTOR (*calling*). Though I warn you, she's got claws…

CLIVE. Here, kitty-kitty!

Beat.

SYLVESTOR (*to* KAREN).…What a horrible little brat.

KAREN. He'll stuff your cat.

SYLVESTOR. Then I guess that's that.

He smiles at the rhyme.

I'm not much of a cat person anyway.

He glances at her, feet.

Oh dear. What happened here? Where are your delicious shoes?

KAREN *looks down at her feet, self-conscious.*

KAREN.…I don't have them any more.

He gasps.

SYLVESTOR. They were stolen?

KAREN *shakes her head.*

They ran away?

KAREN *shakes her head.*

KAREN. They got me in trouble.

SYLVESTOR. Ah.

KAREN. They made me dance.

SYLVESTOR. Good!

KAREN. They made me dance… differently.

SYLVESTOR. Told you!

KAREN. They made everyone angry.

SYLVESTOR. Thought you didn't care what people think.

KAREN. I don't want to make everyone angry.

SYLVESTOR. Oh, my poor little match girl. Watch out for that doormat. Oh, sorry it's you.

He comes closer. She backs away.

Are you saying when you wore them – you didn't love how people looked at you? You didn't revel in the admiration, luxuriate in the envy, slather on the awe… For once they couldn't ignore you. I'll bet they marvelled at all you could do.

KAREN *swallows –*

KAREN. Vanity is a sin.

SYLVESTOR *smiles.*

SYLVESTOR. Vanity schmanity! I see what's in you.

He reaches into his pocket and pulls out a beautiful gold envelope. He offers it to her.

Here…

KAREN. What's that?

SYLVESTOR. An invitation. To a ball. To take place right here in this forest. With the birds and the trees and the VIPS… only those who've been invited can attend. You're invited.

KAREN *opens the envelope.*

Maybe something flies out of it – a butterfly?

Or some glitter falls from the sky.

KAREN *smiles.*

On one condition.

…You wear the shoes.

KAREN *hands him back the invitation.*

KAREN. I told you, I don't have them any more.

SYLVESTOR. But you could find them?

KAREN (*firm*). Mrs Nugent took them.

SYLVESTOR. So take them back.

KAREN (*defiant*). I want Mrs Nugent to like me. I don't want her to send me away.

She looks at him, imploring.

I want to be good.

SYLVESTOR. If only you could.

He smiles.

But you, my dear, don't have a choice

Cos you can hear a different voice

One that's saying – seize this chance

Let the shoes come out and dance

Let them show what you can do

Cos in those shoes, you're more than you

And you know it.

KAREN *shakes her head, wanting to resist.*

In the shoes you're brilliant,

In the shoes you're light

And when you move, it feels so right

Not the orphan no one loves

But a dancer

KAREN. Please –

SYLVESTOR. – with the stars

The shoes can make you who you are.

Come on, Karen, stop playing nice

You know that passion has a price.

KAREN. What does that mean? What price?

SYLVESTOR (*dismissive*). It's a buy-now, pay-later kind of thing – don't worry about it. Just ask yourself the question… Why shouldn't you?

In the distance, we hear a cat screech desperately.

I'll go rescue Manolo – God knows what the little brute has done to him.

KAREN *tries to hand back the invitation.*

KAREN. Here.

He doesn't take it.

SYLVESTOR. Keep it. You might change your mind…

He looks at her, knowing, then reaches into his pocket –

Oh and – these are for the old woman.

– pulls out a bouquet of pink flowers. Hands them to KAREN.

I do hope her suffering is nearing its end.

He turns and skips off.

Manolo! Where are you, darling?

KAREN *looks at the invitation. Then around at the rest of the forest.*

A cold wind blows. She shivers.

Thirteen

The ENSEMBLE *might appear to do the scene change – humming or singing the mirror song. Do they dress* MARIELLA*?*

As CLIVE *and* BOB*, dressed smartly in tuxedos, carry the mirror into* MAGS*'s bedroom.*

MAGS *is still in bed with a drip.* KAREN *is on one side, tending to her.*

MARIELLA*'s in a fabulous gown – talking excitedly.*

MARIELLA. I can't believe it – it's like a dream. Not only did the chairwoman select me as one of only *nineteen* key speakers for the fundraiser, but she asked me for tips!

MAGS. Tips?

MARIELLA. Fashion tips!

MAGS (*dry*). Course.

MARIELLA. I mentioned I was once a personal stylist – I didn't say where – but she was so impressed. I'm this close to getting on the board, I can feel it!

She looks at MAGS.

Now, Mags, look in the mirror –

MAGS (*resistant*). I don't want to look at myself in that thing.

MARIELLA. It's not about looking at yourself, it's about the affirmations. They speed the healing process up no end.

BOB. Is there any science to that or is it just mumbo-jumbo?

MARIELLA. Bob /

MAGS. It's a waste of time, just says the same thing over and over.

MARIELLA. That's not true – remember what it said to Karen.

CLIVE *looks up, interested.*

CLIVE. What did it say to Karen?

MARIELLA. I forget. And it was clearly rubbish, but still. Anything's worth trying once. We need you back to full health ASAP, Mags, cos honestly the state of this house since you got sick… and we wouldn't want to have to go and get a new housekeeper now would we, Bob?

BOB (*surprised*)….no.

MARIELLA. No.

MAGS. No.

MAGS *sighs resentfully at this veiled threat and gives in.*

Mirror mirror on the wall – how do I look today?

MIRROR. You look great today – Mags!

MARIELLA. Marvellous!

MAGS. I hate that thing.

MARIELLA *ignores her.*

MARIELLA (*to* KAREN). She's to do it twice more before bed.

KAREN *nods.*

CLIVE. Hey, Mags, if you die – will you donate your organs to me to make sculptures?

BOB. For God's sake, Clive, that's no way to talk. Mariella, come on – earlier we get there, earlier we can get out. And I like the stuff on sticks. You – come on!

BOB *yanks* CLIVE *out of the room.*

MARIELLA *fixes her hair one last time in the mirror.* KAREN *tentatively approaches.*

KAREN. You look very pretty, Mrs Nugent.

MARIELLA *stiffens.*

MARIELLA. Don't.

KAREN. I was just –

MARIELLA. I know what you were doing. Fool me once, shame on you. But fool me twice – I'll burn you.

KAREN *shrivels back, afraid*. MAGS *tries to distract her.*

MAGS. I'm sure it'll be a beautiful night, Mrs Nugent. Will there be music?

MARIELLA. Of course there'll be music. There'll be ice sculptures and fairy lights and tablecloths made of marshmallows…

MAGS/KAREN (*amazed*). Tablecloths made of marshmallows…

MARIELLA. This fundraiser is world famous. They stint on nothing.

MAGS *looks at* KAREN, *clearly feeling sorry for her.*

MAGS. …And you're sure you wouldn't like to take Karen with you?

MARIELLA. Karen!

MAGS. …Could be good for the speech. You could point at her from the stage – there's the orphan we rescued from the jaws of a – shark-type thing.

MARIELLA. I'm not risking my position with Save the Orphans over an orphan. She almost ruined all my years of good networking.

MAGS. But –

MARIELLA (*over her*). Stop worrying about Karen and get some rest, Mags. She's like a centipede that one, always finds some way to creep on. (*To* KAREN.) We'll be late, don't wait up.

KAREN *nods*.

MARIELLA *glances at the mirror.*

And that mirror is not for you!

KAREN *shrinks back*. MARIELLA *flounces out.*

MAGS *looks at her, sympathetic.*

MAGS. …You would have liked to have gone to that party, wouldn't you? With the marshmallow tablecloths?

KAREN *tries to put a brave face on it.*

KAREN. I don't mind.

MAGS. Don't know how many parties there have been over the years that I would've liked to have gone to, only nobody asked.

She shudders.

KAREN. You're shivering... Are you cold, Mags?

MAGS. It's just my age.

KAREN. I'll get you a blanket.

KAREN *goes to the wardrobe. Opens it.*

There sitting on the shelf are the red shoes.

She gasps.

MAGS. What is it?

KAREN *shuts the door quickly.*

KAREN. Nothing... I saw a spider.

MAGS *frowns.*

MAGS. A spider?

KAREN. There's no blankets in there.

MAGS. Never mind. I'm sure I'll warm up soon enough.

KAREN *thinks.*

KAREN. What about... this?

Then KAREN *reaches into her dress and pulls out the red scarf.*

MAGS. What's that? Is that Mrs Nugent's?

KAREN. No.

MAGS. You mustn't go rooting through her things, Karen. She's like a bloodhound, she'll sniff you out –

KAREN (*suddenly*). It's my mother's.

MAGS *is taken aback.*

MAGS….Oh.

KAREN. Please don't tell Mrs Nugent I have it.

MAGS *takes this in for a beat.*

MAGS….You loved her, didn't you? Your mother.

KAREN *nods sadly.*

Course you did…

MAGS *looks at her, mulling.*

…I had a little girl once. She loved me too… I think. Her father didn't. Ran off the first chance he got. In those days, girls like me, with 'gifts' – or sometimes not… we couldn't be mothers by ourselves. They took her off me.

KAREN. To the forest?

MAGS. To somewhere… never saw her again. She'd be older now of course, my daughter. But I hope wherever she is – she's having a grand old time, and that she was spoiled rotten by her new mother and treated like a queen.

KAREN….I hope so too.

MAGS *looks at* KAREN. *Perhaps they both sense this isn't likely.*

KAREN *puts the scarf around* MAGS*'s neck.*

MAGS. I'll keep this safe for you. Don't worry.

MAGS *lies back in bed, feeling weak.*

…think I need a little sleep now. We'll have our own party later. Just the two of us. There'll be no marshmallow tablecloths, but maybe you'll dance for me?

KAREN. Dance?

MAGS *closes her eyes, sleepy.*

MAGS….I'd like that.

KAREN *pulls the blankets over* MAGS.

A beat.

KAREN *turns and glances back at the wardrobe.*

Another beat.

Then, very tentatively, she walks towards it. Opens the doors.

The shoes are now on a different shelf in a different position – almost teasing her.

MAGS *starts to snore.*

KAREN *shuts the wardrobe doors again. Goes back to* MAGS*'s bed.*

Another beat.

She goes back to the wardrobe.

Both exhilarated and afraid, she gingerly opens the wardrobe doors.

Again, the shoes have moved to a different shelf.

Very slowly KAREN *reaches in and, takes them down.*

She looks at them in her hands.

MAGS *snores.*

KAREN *drops them and quickly goes back to her seat. She picks up a book. Trying to distract herself.*

But the shoes sit behind her.

Do they perhaps start to move towards her?

KAREN *turns around. Looks at them.*

Music – familiar – maybe something we heard with SYLVESTOR *before, trickles gently into the room.*

The golden invitation flutters down from the ceiling.

KAREN *looks around, nervous.*

KAREN. Hello?… Is… someone here?

She looks at the mirror. Then goes towards it.

Mirror mirror, on the wall. How do I look today?

MIRROR (*perfunctory*). You look great today – Karen.

KAREN *stares at her reflection, disappointed.*

She sits back down beside MAGS*'s bed. Picks up her book.*

Then –

You'd look even better if you put on those shoes…

KAREN *jumps in shock. Stares at the mirror.*

KAREN. What did you say?

MAGS *stirs.*

MAGS (*sleepy*).…Karen?

KAREN. Go back to sleep, Mags, it's fine.

KAREN *looks at the shoes.*

MIRROR. What are you waiting for – the old woman's asleep.

KAREN *slowly starts to walk towards the shoes.*

She stops.

Beat.

Go on… What have you got to lose?

KAREN.… nothing. I suppose.

KAREN *looks back at* MAGS, *checking.*

She gingerly steps into one of the shoes.

Then into the other.

She shrugs.

Feels normal.

She starts to walk around.

…Feels fine.

Maybe she does a little skip or something, that turns into a spin.

Feels…

She laughs.

She spins around the room ecstatic.

Mirror mirror, on the wall… How do I look now?

MIRROR. Like the belle of the ball.

Suddenly the wardrobe door opens and KAREN *sees a beautiful dress hanging inside.*

She rushes to the wardrobe and takes it down.

She holds the dress up to herself. Then looks in the mirror.

KAREN….I can't.

MIRROR. Why not?

KAREN. I'm meant to stay here…

MIRROR. It's just this once… Why shouldn't you wear them one more time?

KAREN *picks up the invitation. Glances at* MAGS.

KAREN. I *could…* just go for an hour. She won't even be awake by then.

KAREN *picks up an old-fashioned alarm clock by the bed. Starts to wind it.*

I can set an alarm, make sure I'm back time.

KAREN *quickly puts the dress on, glancing at* MAGS.

I won't be long, Mags, really. And when I'm back – I'll dance for you. I promise.

KAREN *goes to the bed.*

Why shouldn't we get to go to parties, Mags? Why shouldn't we get to go to balls? We're not invisible…

She kisses MAGS *on the forehead.* MAGS *groans in her sleep.*

KAREN *looks at herself in the mirror one last time.*

…Why shouldn't I?

Faint strains of music somewhere, off.

KAREN *picks up the golden envelope.*

She glances at MAGS *one more time, then goes.*

In the bed, MAGS *stirs, slightly distressed in her sleep.*

MAGS (*sleepy, weak*)....Karen?... Karen? I feel a bit... hot. I think I need a glass of... Karen?... Are you there, love?

But KAREN *doesn't reply.*

In the mirror behind her, perhaps we see a brief flash of SYLVESTOR *grinning. There one minute. And then gone.*

Fourteen

The forest. Dark shadows, trees, music. A disco ball?

The ENSEMBLE *appear, dressed to kill. They dance.*

At some point KAREN *emerges from the crowd, exhilarated, excited. She's in the red shoes and in her element. A young man,* PRINCE, *is behind her – he's following her. Eventually –*

PRINCE. Excuse me but... who *are* you?

KAREN *turns, surprised.*

I saw you dance. I'm Prince.

He puts out his hand. She shakes it.

KAREN (*shocked*). Seriously?

PRINCE. My parents loved *Purple Rain*. What's your name?

KAREN....Karen.

PRINCE. Where are you from?

KAREN. The other side of the forest.

PRINCE. How come I've never seen you before?

KAREN. Maybe you have.

PRINCE. I think I'd remember... You're a really good dancer.

KAREN looks at him, shy.

KAREN. It's my shoes.

PRINCE (*surprised*). Your – shoes?

KAREN. They're magic.

A beat. Then PRINCE *laughs.*

PRINCE. Course they are… Will you dance with me?

He takes her hand. They begin to dance.

Something between them. A chemistry.

Behind them – the ENSEMBLE *dance too. As they dance:*

How did you hear about this?

KAREN. He invited me.

PRINCE. Who?

KAREN. The shoemaker.

PRINCE. What shoemaker?

KAREN. He made the invitations.

KAREN reaches into her dress. Pulls out the gold invitation.

But as she does maybe KAREN *and the* PRINCE *are surrounded and separated.*

Maybe the stage gets darker. KAREN *looks around confused.*

She finds herself dancing with SYLVESTOR *for a moment. He snatches the invitation.*

Hey!

And then he's gone.

PRINCE *appears.*

PRINCE. Thought I'd lost you…

They continue to dance.

You were saying something about a shoemaker…

She points to her shoes.

KAREN. He made these… for a dancer who died.

PRINCE. How did she die?

KAREN. I don't know.

PRINCE. Was it gruesome?

KAREN. I don't know.

PRINCE. Was she as amazing as you?

KAREN. I don't know.

She pulls away from him, suddenly insecure.

Why are you talking to me? This is place is full of pretty girls.

PRINCE. So?

KAREN. So why aren't you talking to them?

PRINCE. Because I want to talk to you…You're different.

And suddenly KAREN *deflates.*

KAREN. You mean weird?

PRINCE *laughs.*

PRINCE. I mean it as a compliment. The girls here are all the
    same. Yeah they're good-looking. But that's not
    everything… that's not what I'm looking for.

He looks at KAREN. *Music. He breaks into song.*

Prince's refrain: 'Ordinary Extraordinary Girl'.

> Another night,
> Another ball
> Another evening making small
> Talk
> With girls
> With perfect skin
> And oh so thin
> They could just blow away
> In the wind.

Another night
Another moon
Another pretty lass
To spoon-
Feed – Conversation
Running dry

I don't know why
Makes me want to stab myself
In the eye.

He takes KAREN's *hand, looks at her soulfully.*

I want something deeper
I want someone true
Doesn't matter what she looks like
I don't care if she's… blue
Perfect hair
Shiny teeth.

He grimaces.

(Who cares)
What about
What's underneath
An Ordinary
Extraordinary
Girl
Is who
I want to meet.

Does the music pick up here and he and KAREN *dance as he sings?*

I want someone dazzling
Because of who she is inside
A girl who's some talent
But who's also got a mind
Not a rebel
Not a cheat
A girl who'll sweep me off my feet
An ordinary
Extraordinary
Girl.

Do the ENSEMBLE *join this bit?*

> (It's true)
> An ordinary
> Extraordinary
> Girl
> (That's who)
> An ordinary
> Extraordinary
> Girl
> (Like you)
> Is who
> I want
> To meet.

KAREN *is utterly charmed. They move closer. About to kiss.*

Suddenly the alarm in KAREN's *dress goes off. It startles her.*

They spring apart.

KAREN. Oh no… I have to go.

PRINCE. Now?

KAREN. Someone's waiting for me.

PRINCE. But we've only just met.

> SYLVESTOR *appears.*

SYLVESTOR. Don't leave yet.

He takes KAREN's *hand, pulls her away from* PRINCE. *He dances with her.*

Throughout the following, KAREN *is passed between* PRINCE *and* SYLVESTOR –

The night is young. In fact it's only just –

She's dancing with PRINCE.

PRINCE. – begun. There's so much about you I want to find out.

She smiles.

KAREN. I promised –

PRINCE. Just stay for a little while. Another hour.

And she's dancing with SYLVESTOR.

SYLVESTOR. Why not two? Or three. Or four?

And she's dancing with PRINCE.

PRINCE. What's the worst that can happen? Is your carriage going to turn into a pumpkin?

And she's dancing with SYLVESTOR.

SYLVESTOR. Why are you dancing with that country bumpkin?

KAREN. I have to go. I promised Mags.

She's dancing with PRINCE.

PRINCE. Who's Mags? Your mum?

KAREN*'s getting confused.*

KAREN. No. My mother's dead.

She's dancing with SYLVESTOR.

SYLVESTOR. So get her out of your head.

You're here because you want to live

And the shoes have got so much to give

They're tired of nice

They're tired of quiet

Now they're free – they want a riot.

KAREN *pushes him away.*

KAREN. No!

And she's looking at PRINCE, *who seems shocked at her outburst.*

PRINCE.…Sorry.

KAREN (*confused*). No I'm sorry /

PRINCE. I didn't mean to /

KAREN. It's not you… it's just…

She puts her hand to her head.

My head… I feel strange. I should go.

PRINCE. At least give me your number.

And she's dancing with SYLVESTOR.

SYLVESTOR. Don't you dare!

She pulls away from him.

KAREN. I'm going home.

SYLVESTOR. You wanted to dance.

KAREN. I have danced.

SYLVESTOR. You wanted people to look at you.

KAREN. I – know but /

SYLVESTOR. I made myself very clear. If you come to the ball, you have to stay.

KAREN.… You never said that.

SYLVESTOR. The shoes are out – they want to play.

KARE   But you never said –

SYLVESTOR. I said that passion has its price.

KAREN. But I don't know what that means.

SYLVESTOR. Of course you do…

He comes towards her, sinister.

Deep down. You know exactly what it means.

KAREN *tries to get away. Once again he blocks her.*

She's getting scared.

It's just you want it every way, Karen.

To be the good girl at the Nugents

To be the bad girl here

But that's not how it works, my dear

In every choice

There's something to lose

If you don't choose, the shoes will choose.

He leans down and touches her feet.

And they're such pretty dancing shoes…

Suddenly KAREN *staggers backwards.*

She tries to move forward but can't. She looks at him, helpless.

KAREN.…What's happening?

The shoes start to 'dance' her across the stage.

KAREN *looks around helpless.*

She panics.

Make them stop!

SYLVESTOR. This is what you wanted, Karen. To dance. The shoes are simply giving you what you want.

The shoes move her again.

KAREN. I didn't want this.

He laughs.

The stage gets darker.

The ENSEMBLE *and* SYLVESTOR *back away into the trees.*

(*Terrified.*) Please! Wait! Where are you going?

KAREN *tries to move one way, but the shoes move her the other.*

She tries to move left, but the shoes move her right.

PRINCE *appears.*

PRINCE. Karen?

KAREN. Prince! Help me.

She tries to move towards him. But the shoes move her away.

PRINCE. What's wrong?

She puts out her hands.

KAREN. Take my hands.

He thinks it's a joke.

PRINCE. What?

KAREN. Please!

PRINCE *takes her hands, but the shoes keep pulling*
KAREN *backwards away from him.*

PRINCE (*bemused*). What's happening?

KAREN. Hold on!

But the shoes keep pulling her.

PRINCE. I'm trying but…

KAREN. Don't let me go, Prince! Please don't let me go.

PRINCE *tries to keep holding but the shoes keep pulling*
her –

PRINCE. I can't /

And suddenly KAREN *flies backwards.*

KAREN. Nooooo!

The shoes dance KAREN *away and off. Her voice becomes*
an echo.

PRINCE *stares after her, stunned. Bemused. Afraid?*

PRINCE. Karen?

He starts to follow.

….Karen!

He looks around confused.

Where did she go?

But she's gone.

Fifteen

Music. A loud, cold wind, blows.

We're deep in the forest. Strange noises, screeching owls. Shadows.

Are there gravestones?

The shoes are 'pulling' KAREN along. Dancing her. She's exhausted.

KAREN (*desperate*). Stop. Please, let me stop.

> *She tries to take the shoes off. She pulls and pulls.*

> I didn't want this.

> *Suddenly KAREN hears laughter echoing around her. Voices.*

> *She looks around frightened.*

> Who's there?

> *The VOICES start to mimic her.*

VOICES (*multiple*). Who's there?

> SHADOWY FIGURES *begin to move around her.*

KAREN (*desperate*). Stop it!

VOICES. Stop it.

> *Horrible laughter. Then voices from other times echo around her.*

VOICE 1. Ungrateful girl! /

VOICE 2. Just like her mother /

VOICE 8. She's got sin running through her veins.

> *More laughter.*

> KAREN *looks around desperate.*

KAREN. Please. Just tell me… who's there?

> *From somewhere behind a scrim,* BOB *and* MARIELLA *appear.*

They're at some kind of party. They're dancing. They seem far away, oblivious.

KAREN *tries to go to them.*

Mr and Mrs Nugent!

But the shoes stop her.

(*Calling to them.*) Please! I'm over here!

The shoes keep dancing her away.

VOICES (*mocking*). Please I'm over here!

KAREN. Help!

VOICES. Help!

BOB *and* MARIELLA *disappear.*

The SHADOWY FIGURES *surround* KAREN *pulling at her frightening her.*

Suddenly from somewhere else, another voice.

MAGS. Karen!

KAREN. Mags?

Maybe MAGS *now appears behind the scrim in her bed.*

She's ill.

MAGS (*calling*). Karen, where are you?

KAREN. I'm here, Mags!

MAGS. I don't feel well, Karen.

KAREN. I'm here!

KAREN *tries to go to* MAGS *the shoes and the* SHADOWY FIGURES *stop her.*

Please let me go to her. She needs me.

KAREN *falls. She reaches towards* MAGS.

Mags!

But MAGS *disappears.*

The lights change again.

Day moving into night. Night moving into day.

The wind howls.

The SHADOWY FIGURES *pick* KAREN *up – the shoes making her dance.*

Maybe they chant?

VOICES. Dance, dance, dance – till you drop

Dance, dance, dance – you can't stop

Dance dance dance – till you cry

Dance dance dance – till you die.

KAREN. I want to go home. Please! Let me go home.

The chanting continues.

More VOICES *around her, disembodied.*

VOICE 1. They'll put manners on you where you're going /

VOICE 3. Your mother learned that the hard way /

VOICE 5. With half the men in town knocking on her door /

VOICE 8. She's got sin running through her veins.

More laughter.

VOICES. Dance, dance, dance – all alone

Dance till the flesh is hanging from your bones

Dance through the madness, dance through the pain

Dance till they find you lying your grave.

KAREN *covers her ears.*

KAREN. Stop. Please stop.

The chanting continues as a coffin is carried through the auditorium.

The PRIEST *and* BOB *and* MARIELLA *are at the front, walking sombrely.*

VOICES. Dance dance dance – through your fears

Dance dance dance – through your tears

Dance dance dance – your last breath

Dance dance dance – till your death.

KAREN sees it.

She tries to go to it.

KAREN (*desperate*). Who's dead? Who is it…

But again the shoes or the SHADOWS won't let her.

Is it my mother? /

The PRIEST speaks in a low mutter

PRIEST. In the name of the father and of the son and of the Holy Spirit we commit Margaret Sullivan to the peace of the grave /

KAREN. Mags! No. Please not Mags! /

They don't hear her. They PRIEST continues

PRIEST. From dust you came, from dust you shall return. Christ is the resurrection, the truth and the life /

KAREN. Mr and Mrs Nugent! Please!

PRIEST. Lord God the Holy Spirit have mercy on us. At the moment of death and on our last day, save us, merciful and gracious Lord –

The coffin moves through the auditorium and out.

As it does KAREN reaches out, shattered.

KAREN (*crying*).…I was going to come back. I tried to come back.

KAREN falls to her knees.

The shoes or the SHADOWS make her get up, make her dance. They keep chanting.

No, please. Let me stop.

But they don't.

The lights change, dark to light, light to dark.

KAREN*'s haggard, desperate, falling – her voice a whisper.*

I'm so tired…

The VOICES *mimic her.*

VOICES. I'm so tired.

KAREN. Please.

VOICES. Please.

SYLVESTOR*'s laughter echoes around her.*

SYLVESTOR. If you don't choose, the shoes will choose.

In the shadows we see someone else moving.

Footsteps. Someone coming towards her. The shadow of an axe thrown up on the wall.

KAREN *panics.*

KAREN. No, no…

But the shoes won't let her run.

CLIVE *appears, holding a dead rabbit and some rope.*

CLIVE. You're in trouble.

KAREN.… Clive?

CLIVE. Mags is dead. Everyone's been looking for you. Where've you been?

KAREN. I don't know… Help me, please.

He looks at her. Then around.

CLIVE. Does anyone know you're out here?

She shakes her head. Still 'dancing', desperate.

He lifts the axe, threatening.

So I can do whatever I want …

He comes towards her with the axe. Slow, menacing.

And suddenly KAREN *sees her chance.*

KAREN.…Yes! Yes you can.

CLIVE *falters, suddenly unsure.*

CLIVE. What?

KAREN. Do it!

He stares at her, shocked.

CLIVE.…What?

KAREN. Cut my feet off. The shoes won't stop any other way.

CLIVE *looks at her feet.*

CLIVE. You want me to… cut your feet off?

KAREN (*urging*). Yes!

CLIVE. Seriously?

KAREN. Hurry!

CLIVE *hesitantly raises the axe, takes a step towards her.*

The shoes dance KAREN *a few steps back.*

CLIVE *steps forwards again.*

The shoes dance KAREN *a few steps back…*

CLIVE. You have to stay still.

KAREN. I can't!

CLIVE. I can't get the angle right…

CLIVE *looks around trying to think.*

Here.

He pulls KAREN *behind a tree – behind a screen?*

He gets some rope and ties her to a tree – her feet on the ground.

Now… Are you ready?

KAREN. Yes.

CLIVE. Sure?

KAREN. Yes!

CLIVE *lifts up the axe.*

CLIVE. Okay, on the count of three –

KAREN. Just do it!

CLIVE. Okay!

CLIVE *takes a breath.*

He lifts the axe again.

Then he brings it down on one of KAREN*'s feet.*

THWACK.

KAREN *screams.*

Sounds – birds, wings flapping, screeching, echoing across the forest.

CLIVE *suddenly seems horrified at himself.*

Are you alright?

KAREN. The other one. Hurry!

CLIVE. Okay.

CLIVE *lifts up the axe again. Hesitates.*

Then he brings it down again.

THWACK.

KAREN *screams again.*

More birds' wings flapping, screeching.

CLIVE *looks like he's going to be sick.*

Oh my God… I just – cut your feet off.

He wipes his face and quickly unties the rope.

KAREN. Is it over, Clive? Are the shoes gone?

Suddenly the sound of laughter all around them.

The shoes get up and start dancing before their and our eyes.

CLIVE. What's happening?

   CLIVE *covers his mouth in shock*.

   KAREN *stares at the shoes, dancing in front of her*.

   Should I call for help?

   SYLVESTOR*'s laughter can be heard above them*.

   Karen?

   KAREN *faints*.

   Karen! Are you alright? Karen!

   Darkness.

Sixteen

The sound of sirens mixed somewhere with the strains of a children's choir singing a Christmas carol.

BOB *and* MARIELLA *with collection boxes for the 'Save the Orphans Foundation', step onto the stage*. BOB *is wearing a Santa hat*.

Other than that, they are very serious.

They sing – in the style of a 1940s Christmas movie.

'An Orphan is Not Just for Christmas'.

BOB.
   An orphan is not just for Christmas
   An orphan is not just for fun
   An orphan has feelings
   Like you and I have feelings
   Even if that orphan can't run.

MARIELLA.
   An orphan is not just for Christmas
   An orphan is not for New Year

We took her in
So her life could begin
How did we end up here?

BOTH.
All we wanted to do was help her
All we wanted to do was care.

BOB.
But some people are far beyond helping.

BOTH.
They'd make you tear out all your hair.

MARIELLA.
An orphan is not just for Christmas
An orphan is not just for tea.

BOB.
You can't give them back
Even if you want to give them back.

BOTH.
So please give generously
An orphan is not just for Christmas
For good or for ill
You pay their medical bills.
So please give generously.

MARIELLA. The buckets are at the end of your seats, ladies and gentlemen.

They go.

Seventeen

The Nugents' house. KAREN*'s bedroom.*

MARIELLA, BOB *and the* PRIEST.

They talk in hushed tones outside KAREN*'s room. Perhaps her bed is shrouded in some way so we can't see her.*

MARIELLA. So good of you to come, Father. She hasn't had many visitors.

BOB. Any.

MARIELLA. No.

PRIEST. It's the least I could do, Mrs Nugent. Whole town's been praying for our Karen these past few weeks. How is she?

MARIELLA *glances at* BOB.

MARIELLA. She's – well. Isn't she, Bob? She's doing – well. Considering.

BOB. Been quiet as a mouse since she came back from hospital. Barely eats… And she's smaller now of course, so…

BOB *laughs nervously.* MARIELLA *shoots him a look.*

PRIEST. And she's not been any trouble?

MARIELLA. Oh no. No trouble at all.

PRIEST. Cos if you're finding it too much, there are places…

BOB (*quickly*). Are there? Places that would take her?

MARIELLA. Don't be stupid, Bob. What would people say?

She looks at the PRIEST.

Everyone's blaming us of course – even the Foundation.

BOB. Specially the Foundation.

MARIELLA. I'm not fit for the board apparently. Which is very unfair. Because Clive is adamant she asked him to do it. Practically begged him, he says.

PRIEST. Indeed.

MARIELLA. He's been utterly traumatised by the whole affair. Hasn't made a piece of art since.

MARIELLA looks at the PRIEST, worried.

You don't think she'd have a case, do you?

PRIEST. A case?

BOB. A legal case. For compensation or something.

PRIEST. Oh I doubt it – an unreliable father, a mother who was…

He makes a 'crazy' gesture.

Best compensation for Karen is the forgiveness of our Lord.

MARIELLA. That's a relief.

PRIEST. And I'll be sure to remind her of it too. In case she gets any ideas.

He holds up a collection box – jiggles it.

We're collecting ourselves you know. For the church.

MARIELLA. Yes, yes of course –

MARIELLA nudges BOB, who reaches into his pocket and takes out some money.

BOB. Of course – will a hundred do?

MARIELLA goes to the door of KAREN's room, calls gently.

MARIELLA. Karen, sweetheart. There's someone here to see you.

Lights up on KAREN sitting listless in the bed.

A small Christmas tree with lights twinkles beside her.

The PRIEST steps in.

PRIEST. Hello, Karen. What a lovely Christmas tree. I see the Nugents have been spoiling you.

MARIELLA. Well, we thought it'd cheer her up. There's bells, there's reindeers –

BOB. There's a Santa's stocking for the end of the bed.

He holds it up.

KAREN *flinches, afraid.*

MARIELLA. For God's sake, Bob, could you be more insensitive?

BOB (*bewildered*). What?

MARIELLA (*whispering*). It's red.

BOB. Sorry. I always forget.

MARIELLA. At any rate, it's bit of Christmas spirit to lift the mood. Do your spirits feel lifted, Karen?

KAREN *looks sadly at the tree.*

Course they do!

PRIEST. And I've brought a little gift for you too, Karen.

He holds up a gift.

Have you been saying your prayers?

KAREN *nods.*

Good girl.

KAREN. I pray to God to let me swap places with Mags. So that she can come back and I can die instead.

PRIEST. Oh.

BOB. That's a bit dark.

PRIEST. Yes – better to pray for forgiveness instead. The Lord is merciful, Karen – sure didn't he leave you the rest of your legs?

MARIELLA. He did indeed!

KAREN *opens the present. A Bible.*

KAREN. Thank you, Father.

The NUGENTS *stand a little awkward.*

MARIELLA. And there's more exciting news. Bob and I have had some discussions with some very eminent specialists and by all accounts there are some excellent prosthetics on the market these days.

KAREN. Prosthetics?

MARIELLA. For your feet. Only thing is –

BOB. They're pretty pricey.

MARIELLA. And what with Clive's psychotherapy /

BOB. And the casino getting axed.

MARIELLA. We're a little bit –

BOB. Stretched.

MARIELLA. But in the meantime, Bob and I have found a wonderful man who makes pegs.

KAREN. Pegs?

MARIELLA. Show her, Bob.

BOB *goes to a carrier bag. Pulls out a wooden peg.*

BOB. Here.

KAREN.…What's that?

MARIELLA. Well, they're like little wooden feet I suppose.

KAREN. They don't look like feet.

BOB. As good as.

MARIELLA. They come in different colours.

BOB. Yes. There's blue, there's green, there's –

He pulls out a red. MARIELLA *stops him.*

MARIELLA. Not that one /

He puts it back.

BOB. Green.

MARIELLA. You're spoiled for choice! He'll do a fitting any time – we can have them for Christmas. Aren't they cheerful?

PRIEST. Wouldn't mind a pair myself!

> MARIELLA *and the* PRIEST *laugh a little too loudly.*

> KAREN *stares at them silence.*

MARIELLA. Losing your feet is no reason to lose your manners, young lady.

KAREN. People will laugh at me.

MARIELLA. No they won't.

KAREN. They'll look at me differently /

MARIELLA. Don't be silly.

KAREN. They already do.

MARIELLA. Who looks at you differently?

KAREN. Mr Nugent.

BOB (*shocked*). What?

KAREN. You don't look at me the way you used to.

> MARIELLA *looks at* BOB, *suspicious.*

MARIELLA. And what way was that?

BOB. No idea. Must be the painkillers talking. Can I get anyone a drink?

PRIEST. I'd love a sherry if it's going.

BOB. Sherry. Coming up. Mariella – would you?

MARIELLA. No.

BOB. Right – so.

> BOB *goes, sheepishly.*

> *An awkward silence as* MARIELLA *processes.*

PRIEST. Well… I hear it's going to snow this Christmas. You'll be able to go outside and make snowmen, once you've got your… pegs.

KAREN. I'm not going outside.

MARIELLA. Karen.

KAREN. I'm never going outside again.

MARIELLA. How many times do I have to say it – there's nothing out there.

KAREN. Can I ask a question, Father?

PRIEST. Of course, Karen.

KAREN. When did they realise my mother was crazy?

PRIEST. What do you mean?

KAREN. Like… when was she diagnosed?

PRIEST. Diagnosed? Well, she wasn't – (diagnosed.) Not medically. But her manner, the exuberance, the *dancing* – everyone knew she wasn't right. Normal people don't behave like that.

MARIELLA. No

KAREN *frowns*.

KAREN. But… isn't that why she died?

PRIEST. Good heavens, no. She had a tumour. Didn't she tell you?

KAREN *shakes her head*.

Probably didn't want to worry you. Even the weakest mothers will shield their young.

KAREN *takes this in*.

KAREN. But then –

MARIELLA (*cutting her off*). That's quite enough morbid talk for one day I think. We don't want you upsetting yourself again, Karen. Here take your pills – there's a good girl.

She stuffs a pill into KAREN'*s mouth*.

Come along, Father. Let's leave her in peace.

The room begins to go darker.

Moving slowly into something strange and dreamlike.

KAREN (*worried*). Where are you going?

MARIELLA. You need to get some rest.

KAREN (*scared*). Please don't leave me alone –

MARIELLA. Don't be ridiculous, Karen, we've been through all this. There's nothing to be afraid of. Shoes do *not* get up and walk by themselves!

MARIELLA rolls her eyes at the PRIEST *at they leave.*

The PRIEST*'s voice is heard, loud and echoey around the room.*

PRIEST. Poor girl. What's to become of her?

KAREN sits in the darkness.

Laughter.

SYLVESTOR*'s – it echoes around the room.*

KAREN grips her bed covers, terrified.

She looks around.

Do we see the shoes appear for a moment somewhere in a corner maybe?

And then disappear.

Do we see a flash of SYLVESTOR *sitting beside the bed stroking a toy cat?*

There one minute there, the next gone.

More darkness.

KAREN opens her eyes.

MAGS is sitting in SYLVESTOR*'s place, wearing the red scarf.*

She shakes her head.

MAGS. Poor love. What have you done to your poor feet?

KAREN (*sleepy*)....Mags?... Is that you?

MAGS. Mine are so much better these days… I'm not tortured with my corns any more. And look!

MAGS *kicks her heels. She's wearing red shoes.*

Never knew I had such fabulous legs.

She laughs.

It echoes around the room.

KAREN *shrinks back, afraid of the shoes.*

What? They're only shoes, Karen. They can't hurt you – no matter what that Sylvestor says. You know I'm starting to think he's just clever marketing.

KAREN.…I meant to come back, Mags. I meant to look after you.

MAGS. Why should you be looking after an old woman? You're a child. It's them that should have been looking after you.

MAGS *comes towards the bed, strokes* KAREN's *face.*

Nothing can hurt us now, dear. We've been through the worst. We don't have to keep our heads down any more.

MAGS *lifts up the blanket and looks at* KAREN's *feet.*

She tuts.

Just a pair of old stumps…

MAGS *shakes her head, but she's not shocked.*

Oh well. You'll just have to find some other way to dance now.

KAREN. I'll never dance again, Mags.

MAGS. Don't be silly. You've a gift.

MAGS *comes closer.*

If I don't need eyes to see things…

MAGS *takes the scarf off and puts it around* KAREN's *neck.*

…you don't need feet to dance.

MAGS *kisses her and turns and goes.*

KAREN *tries to hold onto her, but can't.*

KAREN. Where are you going? Mags? Please don't go! Mags! Mags!

But MAGS *does.*

Darkness.

CLIVE *is standing by* KAREN*'s bed. He holds something behind his back.*

CLIVE. Were you having a nightmare? You were shouting in your sleep.

KAREN.…I saw a ghost.

CLIVE. Oh… I'm not supposed to be in here. The lawyer said. But I wanted to give you these.

He holds out some flowers.

To say sorry. For – cutting off your feet.

KAREN *takes the flowers, surprised.*

KAREN. Thought you liked chopping things up.

CLIVE. What's the point of chopping things up if you can't sew them back together again?

He looks sad.

I don't want to chop things up any more. I'm going to become a surgeon. I have the skills. And I can practise on cats.

KAREN. Wow.

CLIVE. Yeah.

He looks down towards her feet.

…Can you still feel them?

KAREN. What?

CLIVE. Your feet. There are all these medical studies of amputees who lost their legs or their arms or their feet.

But they can still feel them. Like if they're sitting down they can still feel where their feet would touch the ground, even though there's nothing there any more. They're like… ghost feet.

KAREN.…Ghost feet?

He nods.

CLIVE. Do you think you have those?

KAREN *looks at her feet in the bed. Suddenly* MARIELLA *enters with a glass of orange juice.*

MARIELLA. Rise and shine –

She looks at CLIVE, *horrified.*

Clive! What are you doing in here? You know you're not allowed.

CLIVE. I brought some flowers.

MARIELLA *looks suspiciously at the flowers.*

MARIELLA. Oh. How thoughtful. Don't do it again.

He goes.

MARIELLA *looks at* KAREN.

You know what I think. I think you've been cooped up in this room long enough. No wonder you're seeing things. I'm going to take you outside for a good old-fashioned dose of fresh air –

She stops.

What's that around your neck?

KAREN *feels her neck. She pulls out the red scarf. She looks at it stunned.*

Where did you get that? I threw that away.

KAREN. What?

MARIELLA. It was wrapped round Mags's neck the night she died. Don't know where she got it. Filthy thing riddled with moths. Give it to me.

MARIELLA *moves to take it.*

KAREN *holds on.*

MARIELLA *pulls –*

Let go.

But KAREN *doesn't. A sort of tug-of-war over the scarf.*

Karen!

KAREN.…Why did you leave me with Mags the night she died?

MARIELLA. Excuse me?

KAREN. You knew how sick she was.

MARIELLA. Yes. And you were supposed to take care of her. You agreed to be her carer.

KAREN. And you agreed to be mine.

MARIELLA *lets go of the scarf in shock.*

MARIELLA. What?

KAREN. When you took me in. You said you'd look after me.

MARIELLA. And I did. I fed you, I clothed you, I bought you shoes… it's not my fault you were off gallivanting in the woods the night Mags died. I only hope you've learned your lesson – vanity is a dangerous thing. It was the ruin of your mother.

KAREN. She didn't look at herself in mirrors half as much as you.

MARIELLA *stares at her, shocked.*

MARIELLA. Passion has a price.

KAREN. Why?

MARIELLA.…What?

KAREN. Why does passion have to have a price?… Why does something you love have to cost you? What's wrong with wanting to dance? What's wrong with looking in a mirror? What's wrong with wanting to feel beautiful, or happy or – free?

MARIELLA *considers. A moment of truth.*

MARIELLA. It gives you notions. Notions that, believe me, life will never live up to. Youth fades, ambition's thwarted, your husband doesn't – look at you any more. You were a good dancer, now you have no feet. What use are notions? They only disappoint. Better to face the cold, hard truth.

MARIELLA *reaches for the scarf, once more.*

KAREN *holds onto it.*

MARIELLA *gives up.*

You'll never walk. You'll never dance. You'll never do anything by yourself again. There's no happy ending, Karen. But guess what – it's the same for all of us.

MARIELLA *starts to walk out of the room.*

KAREN.... You thought I was a good dancer?

MARIELLA *stops.*

Before I got the shoes?

MARIELLA. I thought you had – something.

KAREN. Why didn't you tell me?

MARIELLA. Because I knew what harm it could do.

MARIELLA *leaves.*

KAREN *sits on the bed.*

A beat.

Then, with some difficulty, she sits up and swings her bandaged legs out of the bed. She looks at herself in the mirror. Then she wraps the red scarf delicately around her neck.

KAREN *gets hold of some crutches sitting by the bed and with some difficulty, pulls herself up until she's standing.*

The ENSEMBLE *dismantle the room as snow begins to fall.*

Epilogue

The forest.

It's snowing. Beautiful. The faint strains of music.

KAREN, *on crutches, is moving painstakingly through the snow.*

Suddenly a voice behind her –

PRINCE.…Karen? Is that you?

    KAREN *turns.*

KAREN.…Prince?

PRINCE. I've been looking everywhere for you!

    He rushes towards her.

    I didn't know where you went that night. I searched the whole forest, but no one had seen you. I'm so glad you're alright.

    He embraces her, thrilled.

    I couldn't stop thinking about you. I kept hoping for a sign… something that would tell me where you were.

KAREN. That's amazing –

PRINCE. And yesterday, I found it.

KAREN (*confused*). You found – what?

    He reaches into his coat and pulls out a red shoe.

PRINCE. This!

    KAREN *gasps. Moves back.*

    It was just there. Lying in a bush.

    KAREN *stares at the shoe, horrified.*

PRINCE. It's yours, isn't it? It's your magic shoe – the one you told me about. Thought it was like Cinderella or something, I'm looking everywhere for you and then I find your shoe… Guess now I just have to make sure it fits.

He kneels down in front of KAREN, *a sweeping romantic gesture. She tries to stop him.*

KAREN. No, Prince –

PRINCE. Sssh /

KAREN. It's okay /

PRINCE. You'll ruin my big moment – (*Joking.*) So, princess. Will you try on this shoe?

KAREN. Please.

PRINCE *reaches out.*

PRINCE. Give me your foot.

KAREN. Prince –

PRINCE. Here I'll just –

PRINCE *puts his hand on her foot. He feels.*

PRINCE. Hang on – why can't I… where's your…

A beat as he takes a closer look.

Where the hell is your foot, Karen?

He suddenly jumps back horrified.

…Where are both your feet?

KAREN. I had an accident.

PRINCE. An accident?

He looks at her shocked.

KAREN. But it's okay. I'm okay, see? I can move, I can walk – I don't even need feet any more.

PRINCE *looks at the shoe, then drops it in disgust.*

PRINCE. Oh God… I think I'm going to be sick.

KAREN (*hurt*). I thought you didn't care what people look like.

PRINCE. Yeah but I didn't know you were a freak.

KAREN *is stung. He remembers himself.*

(*To* KAREN.) Sorry. That came out wrong – it's just… you just seemed really different that night. You were so happy. And the way you smiled –

KAREN. I can still smile.

She smiles.

PRINCE. But the way you moved.

KAREN. I can still move.

She moves towards him. He moves away.

PRINCE. But the way you were – with your feet.

KAREN. It's still me, Prince.

He backs away from her.

PRINCE. Yeah but who is that really? I mean I don't even know you. We had a dance, I found your shoe – it's hardly grounds for – marriage?

He laughs, awkward.

KAREN *looks at him sadly.*

KAREN.…So you didn't mean what you said… about wanting to meet someone extraordinary?

PRINCE. Well –

KAREN. Cos losing your feet is pretty extraordinary – don't you think?

PRINCE. Yeah.

KAREN. So… you're just not as deep as you thought you were then?

PRINCE.…guess not.

PRINCE *feels stupid.*

You can have your shoe back. If you want.

He holds it out to KAREN.

I have the other one too… thought it'd be more romantic with just the one but – here.

He takes out the other shoe –

Take them.

He puts them on the ground in front of KAREN.

She looks at them.

PRINCE *steps back away from her. Looks at her feet.*

Sorry about your…

He gestures to her feet.

…but Happy Christmas, yeah?

She stares at the shoes.

Oh and be careful out here. Apparently there's like – ghosts in the trees or something…

KAREN*'s still looking at the shoes.*

KAREN.…Ghost feet.

PRINCE. Okay. Yeah.

He makes a 'crazy' gesture to himself and runs off.

KAREN *stares at the shoes. Maybe she pokes one with a crutch.*

KAREN. They're just a pair of shoes…

The snow falls around KAREN.

Mags was right. They're just… shoes.

Beat.

They're nothing.

She looks around. The snow is falling thicker.

It gets brighter. Stranger.

Some music faintly, off.

KAREN *takes off her coat. But maybe keeps the red scarf around her neck.*

Very slowly she begins to move on her crutches.

Then one by one she throws each crutch away and starts to dance.

It's tentative and unsteady at first– as she finds her feet. Maybe some of the ENSEMBLE *come out of the forest or carry her.*

But soon she's dancing – beautiful, delicate, mesmeric.

Suddenly in the distance voices – BOB, MARIELLA, CLIVE.

They're calling for her, genuinely worried.

MARIELLA. Karen!

BOB. Karen, where are you!

MARIELLA. Oh what if something's happened? I shouldn't have lost my temper – she's fragile.

CLIVE. Look, I think I see her!

MARIELLA. Where?

CLIVE. There!

MARIELLA. Karen – you shouldn't be out here in the dark.

They stop.

They stare at KAREN *'dancing'.*

Karen… Oh my.

BOB. What's she doing?

MARIELLA *reaches for* BOB*'s hand.*

MARIELLA. I think… she's… dancing.

BOB. Dancing? How could she be dancing.

MARIELLA. I don't know. But she is. Look.

They look.

It's like…

BOB. Magic…

Stunned, BOB *takes* MARIELLA*'s hand. They watch in wonder as* KAREN *keeps dancing, snow falling all around her.*

BOB *looks at* MARIELLA *and very gently he takes her hand and they too begin to dance. Do* MAGS *and the 'ghosts' appear too?*

As KAREN *continues moving and the lights begin to fade –* SYLVESTOR *walks out onto the stage.*

He holds the curtain and looks at us.

SYLVESTOR. And so we're here

At the end

To see

Our little orphan girl

Transcend

Her limitations

Though it's

Bittersweet

They'll never give her back her feet

Happily Ever After?

Well, there's no plain sailing

But that, my dears

is fairytale-ing

The moral –

Who wants morals?

Life's more than luck

Or chance

Because you make your own fortune

When you dance your own dance.

He steps into the action and into the snow.

He pulls the curtain down.

The End.

A Nick Hern Book

The Red Shoes first published in Great Britain in 2017 as a paperback original by Nick Hern Books Limited, The Glasshouse, 49a Goldhawk Road, London W12 8QP, in association with the Gate Theatre, Dublin

Cover design: iZest Marketing

Designed and typeset by Nick Hern Books, London
Printed in Great Britain by Ashford Colour Press, Gosport, Hampshire

A CIP catalogue record for this book is available from the British Library

ISBN 978 1 84842 713 6

www.nickhernbooks.co.uk

facebook.com/nickhernbooks

twitter.com/nickhernbooks

Our Creatives

Creatives

Director	Selina Cartmell
Set and Costume Design	Monica Frawley
Lighting Design	Paul Keogan
Choreographer	Liz Roche
Composer	Marc Teitler
Associate Director	Maisie Lee
Assistant Designer	Katie Davenport
Stage Director	Clare Howe
Assistant Stage Managers	Lucie Ryan Donnelly
	Emma Coen
Costume Supervisor	Sinead Lawlor
Set Construction	TPS
Photography	Agata Stoinska
Graphic Design	iZest